Effective Human Resource Development

Neal E. Chalofsky
Carlene Reinhart

Chalofsky, Neal

Effective Human Resource Development

How to Build a Strong and Responsive HRD Function

Jossey-Bass Publishers

San Francisco • London • 1988

EFFECTIVE HUMAN RESOURCE DEVELOPMENT
How to Build a Strong and Responsive HRD Function
by Neal E. Chalofsky and Carlene Reinhart

Copyright © 1988 by: Jossey-Bass Inc., Publishers
350 Sansome Street
San Francisco, California 94104
&
Jossey-Bass Limited
28 Banner Street
London EC1Y 8QE

Library of Congress Cataloging in Publication Data

Chalofsky, Neal, date.
    Effective human resource development: how to build a strong and
responsive HRD function / Neal E. Chalofsky, Carlene Reinhart. —
1st ed.
        p.   cm. — (The Jossey-Bass management series)
    Bibliography: p.
    Includes index.
    ISBN 1-55542-081-8 (alk. paper)
    1. Personnel management.   2. Career development.
3. Manpower planning.   4. Organizational effectiveness.
I. Reinhart, Carlene.   II. Title.   III. Series.
HF5549.C435 1988
658.3—dc 19   87-46334
                                                                      CIP

Manufactured in the United States of America

The paper in this book meets the guidelines for
permanence and durability of the Committee on
Production Guidelines for Book Longevity of the
Council on Library Resources.

JACKET DESIGN BY WILLI BAUM

FIRST EDITION

Code 8753

The Jossey-Bass
Management Series

Contents

Preface

American organizations today are experiencing significant turbulence that directly affects human resource development functions. Our society is undergoing what Thomas Kuhn (1962) refers to as a paradigm shift: our working assumptions—the "facts" that govern our lives, that we accept as "truths"—are in conflict with our experiences, creating tension that will eventually force a re-evaluation of those assumptions and the formulation of a new world view. Several years ago we began to realize that many of the "facts" and "truths" that HRD functions have traditionally accepted as standards for performance now are not only irrelevant but may even be counterproductive to organizational effectiveness.

Part of the HRD function is to provide information that will help the organization maintain effective operations now and in the future. Certainly few line organizations can afford the time or money that would be required for working staff to monitor changes, evaluate needs, and make recommendations for improvements. Corporations depend on their HRD functions to do this for them.

As we began to look at various types of HRD functions, it became obvious that they are being challenged daily, and yet there did not seem to be any place for an HRD function to turn, no models for the model-builders, no blueprint for HRD managers to use and be able to say, "If we do it *this* way, we should be able to improve our effectiveness and our organization will in turn thrive."

As human resource development practitioners, we are

deeply concerned about charges and evidence of frequent failures of the HRD function to prepare workers to work or managers to manage. We believe that HRD, properly carried out, may ultimately prove critical to the survival of many organizations. Rosabeth Moss Kanter, in *The Change Masters,* notes that in recent years the business press has given increasing attention to the quality of management and to management actions as a factor in business success, and, she writes, "human resource management has moved from backstage to center stage. . . . The majority of the issues growing in importance concerned human resources" (Kanter, 1983). From the bit parts we HRD practitioners have been used to playing rather comfortably, suddenly here we all are on center stage! The lights go up, the world changes beneath our feet, and too many of us seem to be caught in a chorus line mentality. We *can* help our organizations, at least we believe that we can, but we are not sure what the opening line should be, or even how the stage should be set—and frustration looms large!

We undertook the research that has led to this book because we believe that there is a survival path for organizations and that that path lies at the end of a route which must include a truly effective human resource development function. Our thoughts prior to starting our research went something like this:

- According to many indicators, American industry is in more trouble today than ever before in the history of this country (Dun & Bradstreet, 1982-83).
- The indicators point to human incompetence as the primary reason for declining productivity and increasing business failures (Dun & Bradstreet, 1982-83).
- The charter of *most* HRD functions is to help people become more competent and to help organizations meet their goals.
- If more businesses than ever are failing due to incompetence, then HRD functions are *not* effectively enabling people and organizations to meet their goals; HRD organizations themselves are not functioning effectively.

- Therefore, as HRD practitioners, we must find ways to make the HRD function become more effective at fostering and maintaining the competence of employees and hence of whole organizations.

We believed that a model or process was needed for effective HRD functions. The first step, however, had to be a definition of HRD function effectiveness. Once this was done, we reasoned, we would be able to develop the tools that HRD functions can use to build their own competence, and ultimately the competence of their organizations' people. For the purpose of this book, we define and describe an HRD function as the organizationally based unit responsible for providing planned adult learning activities, services, and programs to members, individual and collective, of the organization, for job or skill training, education, and development.

Moving on from this definition, we have built a knowledge base on which to found our model. This base has eventually grown to include research, an extensive literature review, and interviews with many practitioners.

We present in this book the culmination of three years' work: an HRD practitioner's view of HRD functional excellence. We do not imply that currently popular approaches to organizational development such as organizational leadership (Bennis), "change masters" (Kanter), or even "walking around" and building "skunk works" (Peters) are not viable concepts and practices. They mesh nicely with our findings. What this book provides is a way to look at, assess, and improve the critical HRD function of an organization so that it can in turn provide the services and support needed to build competence in the total organization.

Who Should Read This Book?

This book is for all line and staff managers who are concerned with the effectiveness of their organizations. It will help line managers to work more effectively with the organization's HRD function to achieve organizational survival and growth— to use the available power resources to the greatest advantage.

Of equal importance, this book is the first tool specifically developed to help HRD managers and practitioners assess the effectiveness of their own functions. It is based on the premise that in order to improve anything systematically, one must first know what the improvement should look like. "If you do not know where you are going, you may end up somewhere else."

This book will also be valuable for every person interested in a career in HRD. New or potential practitioners will be able to assess their own desire and ability to carry out HRD activities in this unique, critical, and growing area of American organizational life.

Overview of the Contents

Each chapter of the book is a building block for the chapters that follow. We have not attempted to provide the reader with a discrete blueprint and set of specifications in each chapter, but rather to build a framework through our research findings, interviews, and examples of what successful HRD functions are doing. It will be up to HRD practitioners to adapt the model to the unique needs of their organizations.

In Chapter One we explain the issues that prompted us to write the book and discuss the key issues that it addresses: change linked to visibility and growth of the HRD function; the resultant pressing need for a model for effective HRD function. We present our methodology in Chapter Two, and in Chapter Three we discuss our findings: the key elements of effectiveness identified by the initial Delphi study, and the HRD effectiveness criteria that were identified as a result of the survey and telephone interview phases of our investigations. In Chapter Four, we describe the model we derived from our research that represents the primary goals, criteria, and standards for HRD effectiveness in a format that encourages HRD managers to examine their functions critically. Chapters Five through Seven explain the three primary effectiveness criteria, and present examples that illustrate the criteria put into practice. These vignettes illustrate how HRD professionals in various types of organizations demonstrate effectiveness. Chapter Eight presents a case study of one organization that is working successfully, using the criteria we describe in Chapters Five through Seven. Because we intended our research to be *used* by organizations, not just read and filed away, Chapter Nine puts it all together in a process, the HRD Effectiveness Improvement Process, that we have developed for managers and HRD practitioners to use to evaluate their own HRD functions, identify areas of needed improvement, and develop plans of action. Finally, in Chapter Ten we look at HRD effectiveness for the future. We make predictions, based on our research data, of changes and trends that we believe will affect the HRD function over the next decade.

This book is not intended to serve as *the* answer or to present *all* the answers. We urge you to read it with the idea that you will be able to integrate the information we present with your own knowledge and experience. If you do this, we believe that you will be able to develop a model for HRD functional effectiveness that makes sense for you and your organization.

The book needs to be read consecutively and perceived as a whole, the sum of its parts. HRD effectiveness, as we have conceived it, derives from the interrelationship of activities within an environment; it does not occur as a series of isolated or random events.

Probably one of the most central notions in HRD is *commitment.* All of the ideas and suggestions in this book are for naught unless the people involved in using them are truly committed to effectiveness. You will notice there is no pull-out poster in the middle of the book that you can pin on your office wall that summarizes the major points. There are no quick-fix answers or one-minute concepts: *achieving effectiveness is hard work.*

Acknowledgments

A number of people have made significant contributions to this work: Karen Stacy was an integral part of the first critical elements study; Ronald Zemke of *Training Magazine* helped us obtain a random list of 1,000 HRD managers; Leon Nawrocki of

Xerox Corporation picked up the tab for the first mailing, and even stuffed envelopes; the Woodlands Group provided invaluable pre-Delphi assistance; Florence Smoczynski organized the data from the organizational survey; and Linda Morris, Karen Stacy, Richard Stacy, Caroline Shook, and Lynn Ernst conducted the follow-up interviews. Thom Murray provided a caring critique and a great deal of motivation, and Lane Murray showed us how to do it right—providing a beautiful organizational model as well as inspiration. Last but not least, we thank Bruce Reinhart and Margie Chalofsky, who put up with our working on the research and then the book on "family time."

January 1988   Neal E. Chalofsky
                                                  Takoma Park, Maryland

                                                  Carlene Reinhart
                                                  Vienna, Virginia

The Authors

Neal E. Chalofsky is a visiting assistant professor of human resource development at George Washington University. He received his B.S. degree (1966) from Temple University in personnel management, his M.B.A. degree (1968) from American University in human relations, and his Ed.D. degree (1976) from George Washington University in human resource development.

Chalofsky's main professional and research activities have been in the areas of the professional and career development of HRD specialists and in the improvement of the effectiveness of the organizational HRD function. He has served as chairperson of the American Society for Training and Development's Professional Development Committee, and has served on the HRD Careers Committee, the Future of HRD Task Force, and the HRD Professors Network. He has been involved in every major HRD competency study in the United States and Canada. In 1984, Chalofsky received ASTD's National Torch Award for contributions to the association and profession. His publications include *Up the HRD Ladder: A Guide to Professional Growth* (1983, with Carnie Ives Lincoln), as well as several chapters in books of readings and numerous articles. He has made more than thirty-five presentations to local, regional, national, and international meetings and conferences.

Chalofsky was director of the HRD graduate program at Virginia Polytechnic Institute and State University from 1980 to 1987. Prior to that he held various HRD positions in the National Aeronautics and Space Administration (NASA), the Department of Health, Education and Welfare, and the U.S.

Office of Personnel Management. He has consulted with such organizations as Computer Science Corporation, Arthur Young and Co., the World Bank, the U.S. General Accounting Office, the National Alliance of Business, and Alpha Steel (Mexico).

Carlene Reinhart is manager of computer assisted instruction design, Customer and Marketing Education, U.S. Marketing Group, at Xerox Corporation. She received her B.A. degree (1954) in American diplomatic history, her M.A. degree (1970) in adult education, and her Ed.D. degree (1976) in human resource development, all from George Washington University.

Reinhart has worked for Xerox Corporation since 1980, when she conducted a major performance analysis study of the customer administration function for Rank Xerox, analyzing performance in Xerox Sweden and Xerox Italy. She has held management positions with Xerox Corporation in the United States and abroad and has managed products in customer administration training and training analysis, design and development, applications of artificial intelligence, and computer-based training.

Prior to joining Xerox Corporation, Reinhart spent four years as assistant director of the National Advisory Council on Adult Education (1974-1978), where she conducted national studies of state support for adult education (1977) and designed a competency mapping process for the U.S. Office of Adult Education (1978). She spent five years on the National Board of Directors of the American Society for Training and Development (1978-1983) and holds the Women's Network Professional Development Leadership Award (1981) and the society's Torch Award (1983).

Reinhart has been president of her own company, Commonwealth Learning, Inc. (1968-1974), a national consulting firm specializing in program evaluation and the development and installation of management systems for colleges, universities, and school systems.

Effective Human Resource Development

1

Changing Demands
on the HRD Function

They [the Americans] have all a lively faith in the
perfectibility of man . . . they all consider society as a
body in a state of improvement . . . and they admit
that what appears to them today to be good, may be
superseded by something better tomorrow.
——Alexis de Tocqueville,
Democracy in America,
1935

Several years ago, Bob Dylan recorded a song that appealed to
many of us: "The Times, They Are a-Changing." That expres-
sion has never been more appropriate than it is today. In this
chapter we present the issues that caused us to write this book,
and the issues that emerged as a result of our research. In a
word, it is all about change. We are talking about the linked
issues of visibility and growth, and the compelling need for a
process or model to deal with the problems of increasing effectiveness in the midst of all the change. We discuss changing
attitudes and HRD political relevance, and we present evidence
of concern for HRD effectiveness—a major issue.

From these issues, we move into the next chapter: the
research itself—how we did it, what our findings were, and the
model that has evolved. We present the model, then go on to
provide examples of effective HRD organizations doing the
kinds of things that the model identifies. In these chapters, you
will begin to see how the model can work, and you can identify
the types of actions and activities that will work for you in

1

your specific organization. We have not provided a quantitative model, but rather a framework and examples for you to adapt and adopt or improve upon. Not only would a specifically quantitative model be outdated before this book reaches print in these fast-changing times, it also would not be equally appropriate for any and all organizations. Rather, we have provided an architectural blueprint that allows you, the HRD "general contractor," to decide the specifics of your construction process depending on the resources you have available and the requirements of your clients. An adobe house would be difficult to build, expensive, and probably not too useful in northern Maine.

In reading the case study in Chapter Eight, you will have yet another opportunity to see how one organization orchestrated activities for functional effectiveness within the model's framework. Finally, taking the issues, research, the model, and our examples into consideration, we present you with a process that you can use to improve the effectiveness of your own organization.

Visibility and Growth

Gone are the days when trainers needed only good platform skills to be considered successful, or worried only about whether the course would fill. Gone are the days of training for training's sake. Clearly human resource development (HRD) is no longer a luxury reserved for giant corporations; no longer a reward reserved for productive employees; no longer an activity to keep employees busy during downtime. HRD today is a bottom-line, strategically important part of business enterprise. In some organizations HRD resources are even being considered an asset, not a liability. As the American Society for Training and Development has noted, "Human resource activities are no longer a group of diverse practices on the periphery of a few organizations. The importance to the American economy of work-related learning is at last widely recognized. As organizations return, in turbulent times, to basic questions about their nature and purposes, the contribution of skill and behavior development to corporate performance is clear. Consequently, the field has moved far beyond isolated attempts to teach specific skills to workers to include complex strategic systems for solving critical organizational problems and meeting competitive challenges in the global marketplace" (1986, p. 4).

The recognition that HRD is now receiving is a two-edged sword. On the one hand, awareness of the significance of our activities is long overdue; it is a nice feeling to finally be heard. On the other hand, this recognition means we must live up to our potential; it means we must deliver.

The more visible we become, the more vulnerable we become. HRD in America is becoming too vast in scope to be kept hidden, even if that were our aim. At a White House briefing approximately eight years ago, it was announced that HRD programs within the federal government were a billion-dollar activity, and suddenly the Office of Management and Budget wanted to know how effectively those funds were being used. Today, government HRD is budgeted at approximately $5 billion. Nationwide, total spending for all employee informal and formal training is estimated to be $210 billion per year (American Society for Training and Development, 1986). As we began to discuss visibility and growth (the issues that really started our research), the realization dawned on us that HRD, as a segment of our economy, not only affects a much larger segment but is significant in and of itself—and yet there was no clear definition of success in this $210 billion industry.

We also realized that the visibility of HRD and the very real need for its activities will grow much larger in the next several years. In the 1970s organizations had plenty of competent, qualified talent for most jobs. But by the 1990s, the percentage of women entering the workplace will level off and the "baby boom" males will have moved through the system (American Society for Training and Development, 1986). Competition for qualified employees will be stiff because of the smaller labor pool of entry-level applicants. We are already seeing evidence of this: you can't drive by most retail stores, restaurants, and supermarkets without seeing "employees wanted" notices in the windows. We are having to face the "work smarter" syndrome: corporations are growing in size but carefully, looking for increasingly more competent people. HRD functions themselves may well be faced with a decreasing pool of trained and experi-

enced practitioners in the near future. We will have to become
more efficient and effective in every aspect of our operations.

We looked further at the issue of growth. The Conference
Board, in a study of trends in corporate education and training,
found that the number of training professionals had increased
in nearly two-thirds of the firms surveyed. The board cited the
following as evidence of the enhanced role and status of HRD in
many companies:

- Management has become convinced that education drives the business.
- A stepchild until recently, the training function
  is now seen as essential to the company's strategic goals.
- Developing our people is now the heart of our
  business strategy.
- Training departments used to be wiped out by
  recessions, but few were in the recent one [Lus-
  terman, 1985, p. 2].

Another factor affecting the growth of HRD is the increase
in the overall number of jobs and the shifts from sectors such
as manufacturing to service organizations. Newly created jobs
require new skills training and workers being displaced need
retraining. In addition, more workers are coming to expect training as part of the normal job environment, and will demand it
if they don't see it. This is especially true in high technology,
where employees (and management) want to stay on the leading
edge—they can't afford not to.

Changes in Attitudes. Changes in attitudes, as well as skills
and knowledge, have been necessitated by many companies' adop-
tion of new strategies and goals—responses to heightened global
competition, deregulation, and other changes in the business
environment (Lusterman, 1985). Two examples of industries
where major changes have required a significant amount of
increased training are banks and hospitals. Both are becoming
more competitive, and training in marketing and customer service has intensified dramatically.

A different type of attitude change is found in the increased respect and support for HRD being exhibited by top executives. Many are responding to the issues cited above, but others are reacting to personal experience. We are witnessing the first generation of senior managers raised in supervisory, management, and executive development programs. Ironically, much of the emphasis on HRD in many companies is in the area of management development. Managers are seen as the key to implementing new or revised corporate strategies. Managerial roles are also changing from directing to counseling/coaching.

Organizations will have to rely on HRD to provide the competence and productivity they desperately need. Corporations will actually use HRD services as enticements to attract workers. In 1986, IBM ran a four-page advertisement in *Newsweek* describing how the company provides retraining for its employees. It is time our concern shifts from a survivalist mentality to an effectiveness mentality.

Political Relevance. Last, but not least, HRD has become politically relevant.

> The Democrats need a human resource plank because they are a coalition of separate groups—women, minorities, labor—and they need a unifying concern. They also want to appear to support productivity and not to be seen primarily as consumers of benefits and tax dollars. Their attention is shifting from the disadvantaged person outside the employment structure to the employee within.
>
> The Republicans are interested in productivity improvement programs because it suits their image, as the party of sound business management. By supporting HRD programs they can add to their concern for growth, autonomy, and opportunity within the private sector: a much needed image of concerns for people [American Society for Training and Development, 1986, p. 12].

How such visibility will ultimately affect HRD functional effectiveness is yet unknown. Perhaps we will make wise use of this type of leverage to seek funding for a broad range of badly needed research activities. Perhaps we will be able to influence political programs that maximize the use of public funds for as-yet-undiscovered training needs. One thing is certain: we have come of age and we must accept the requirements for responsible and accountable behavior as a result.

Concern for HRD Effectiveness

Having recognized some of the problems that growth and visibility bring to a field, we determined that our first step had to be identifying criteria for HRD effectiveness. This was not a new idea. In 1980, sixty experts from the HRD field and related disciplines met in Kansas City to attempt to identify the most critical research issues in HRD. Of the eight issues identified, one centered around HRD functions. Here the key research question was, How should the success of HRD programs and organizations be measured (Alden, 1982, p. 71)?

Several authors have proposed sets of criteria for measuring effectiveness. Lippitt (1976), described thirteen criteria for evaluating HRD organizations.

1. Addressing of relevant needs.
2. Clear objectives.
3. Accomplishments.
4. Sensitivity to unique needs of the organization.
5. Flexibility in adapting to changing needs.
6. Skill orientation.
7. Professional leadership.
8. Future prospective.
9. Consistency of values between individual programs and the human system that is served.
10. Evaluation.
11. Information systems.
12. Organizational support.
13. Participation commitment.

Shoemaker (1976) reported on the efforts of a task force at AT&T to evaluate training activities. His group derived sixteen criteria:

1. Accountability.
2. Technological integration.
3. Technological assimilation.
4. Training function integration.
5. Human performance requirements integration.
6. Mission emphasis.
7. Functional expertise.
8. Control.
9. Communications interface.
10. Responsiveness.
11. Flexibility.
12. Effectiveness.
13. Competitive ability.
14. Service capabilities.
15. Management emphasis.
16. Degree of change.

The literature on how to *measure* HRD functional success or effectiveness has been scant; published ideas on how to be more effective have been numerous. Here are two examples of such lists:

Find a need and fill it.
Be action-oriented.
Spend money wisely.
Manage training results and outcomes.
Exhibit positive managerial skills.
Select programs that are effective in changing behavior.
Conduct evaluation studies that convincingly demonstrate results.
Communicate training's accomplishments to the organization (Zenger and Blitzer, 1981).

Proactiveness.
Select actions that are aligned demonstrably with organizational mission.

Assert your human system perspective appropriately.
Develop an action plan and share it with your users.
Follow up on efforts you begin.
Build on small successes.
Be candid with your clients.
Give recognition to others.
Learn from your clients.
Promote informal learning.
Give the client more than expected (Bell, 1984).

Before we go any further, we want to dispel any notions that we are belittling these authors' lists of criteria for measuring or achieving effectiveness. We used many of these lists as a basis for our research. Our objective for sharing this information is twofold: to give you an idea of the literature on this topic and to share the concern that few if any of these lists have been based on *research*.

Useful Research

The last major issue we wanted to address was conducting and presenting useful research in HRD. One of the criticisms of research often heard in our field is that research findings and conclusions are presented in ways that are not really useful to practitioners. One of the criticisms often heard of practitioners is that they are looking for instant tools and fast answers to make their jobs easier. Because we feel both criticisms are often valid, we take what we hope is a balanced approach and provide you with as many answers as possible to key questions, and present these findings in a way that is consistent with the purpose of this book: to develop a model that practitioners can make organization-specific for their own unique uses.

As we read through the literature we started asking ourselves the following questions—which ultimately became the research questions on which the studies were based:

• What is effectiveness? Is it a measure of productivity, efficiency, credibility, or all these? Is it based on hard data or perception?

- What does effectiveness look like? How do you really know when you are effective? Can it be (somewhat) objectively measured? Should it be?
- What does it take to achieve effectiveness? What do successful HRD functions do to be effective?
- Can ineffective HRD functions really improve significantly? How much time, energy, and material resources are needed to be effective?

In the following chapters we tell the story of moving from asking research questions to identifying a useful research methodology; ultimately we present the findings that resulted from our research efforts.

2

Searching for Keys
to HRD Effectiveness:
The Research Study

Knowledge comes, but wisdom lingers.
——Alfred, Lord Tennyson,
"Locksley Hall," 1842

We approached our proposed research with both excitement and trepidation. We were, after all, planning to explore an area that had never really been investigated, and that is exciting. The fear we shared is one acknowledged by many researchers: we might not actually discover anything useful!

Our mutual interests might have led us along other paths, but we chose to conduct research because we felt it was important to solicit from the field of human resource development a broad consensus of opinion and practice, instead of speculating on what we ourselves believe HRD effectiveness to be. We are also committed to the belief that research is a vital element of an emerging profession, and we wanted to be able to demonstrate the utility of conducting an applied, practical research study. This chapter describes our research methods and the demographics of our two surveys.

Research Methodology

Research is essential to the HRD field for a number of reasons: to effectively develop human resources, solve critical organizational problems, identify the scope and breadth of the

10

HRD field, and assist the field in its transformation into a profession. Yet research is a neglected and often maligned activity in HRD. Practitioners do not have time to read research-based articles, HRD functions do not consider many of their data-gathering and inquiry-based studies as research, and many organizations will not share their research for proprietary reasons. To add to the stresses of time constraints and incipient paranoia, there is little incentive in our field to publish research. Practitioners are not rewarded by their organizations for conducting studies and publishing books or articles. Indeed, they may be criticized for taking time away from their jobs! One of the benefits we hope practitioners may gain from this book is an understanding of the significance of research and an interest in conducting research studies. And we hope managers will better understand the need to support the research their HRD personnel seek to conduct.

The first step in any research process is to identify a potential problem or issue in which the researcher is interested enough to want to study further. We identified an issue that we feel is critical to the field, and is also one that interested us personally: what is HRD effectiveness, and how can it be improved?

To organize our thoughts, and also to seek possible funding to support the research, we developed a proposal outlining our research objectives and methodology. The research objectives identified the three specific outcomes we wanted to produce, and the methodology specified the research design we planned to use to achieve them:

1. Generate a list of critical elements of HRD effectiveness.
2. Survey a selected number of organizational HRD functions that meet these critical elements of effectiveness.
3. Identify the characteristics common to these organizational HRD functions.

We identified our research method as a theoretical model-building design, a method described by the American Society for Training and Development (ASTD) research committee in their

1986 publication, *Doing Research in Human Resource Development* (Miller and Barnett). In this method, a hypothetical framework or model is developed out of an ideal set of elements, and this is then used to prescribe the implementation of these elements in the real world. Our bottom line was to develop a model of the "ideal" HRD function, and then to demonstrate how organizations can systematically achieve the elements of the model.

The Delphi Study

We discovered that, given the objectives, we needed to conduct a multi-stage research study. We needed to identify the critical elements of the model; to do that, we needed first to develop a list of possible criteria of effectiveness, then subject that list to a research technique that would result in a list of critical elements. We then needed to identify organizations with internal HRD functions and study those organizations in some way to glean what characteristics effective HRD functions have in common.

We decided to use the Delphi study method for the first stage of our research, and an organizational survey with follow-up telephone interviews for the second stage. The Delphi technique was developed by the Rand Corporation in the early 1950s to obtain group opinion about urgent defense problems (Rossman and Carey, 1973). Basically, it uses questionnaires to collect opinions on a topic anonymously, in an effort to produce a group consensus. The process involves selecting the Delphi panel (a group of people identified by set criteria as "experts" in the field in question) and submitting to them several rounds of questionnaires on the problem until they reach consensus. Initial questionnaires ask the panel to make judgments about lists of items and to include reasons for their judgments. Successive questionnaires ask the panel to revise their judgments by reviewing the comments from the previous questionnaires. Usually three or four rounds are needed to reach the desired level of agreement.

The Delphi technique allows for the collection of expert knowledge and opinion. At the same time, it eliminates costly travel and per diem expenses, avoids the problem of trying to get people with busy schedules together at one time, avoids unproductive conflict at face-to-face meetings, and eliminates the bias that perception of status and expertise might otherwise create.

The central ideas are to eliminate any direct confrontation of the experts, to allow their opinions to be fully independent (because of the anonymity of the panel), and to foster consensus based on relevant information (Tersine and Riggs, 1976).

From a comprehensive search of the literature, we developed a list of 105 possible critical elements. We quickly realized that this was much too unwieldly a list to submit to a Delphi panel, so we asked a prestigious sixteen-member HRD support group, the Woodlands Group, to act as a review team to shrink the list to a more manageable size. The Woodlands Group produced a list of 51 elements. We then selected 105 people from the list of 300 persons previously selected as HRD experts by the ASTD "Models of Excellence" study. The experts we selected were fairly evenly divided into three groups: internal practitioners (in both the public and private sectors), academia, and consultants. We sent them the first round of our Delphi questionnaire, which asked them to rank each element as to its criticalness on a five-point Likert scale. We also asked them to comment on each ranking. Sixty-one respondents identified thirty-two elements as being critical on a basis of comparing weighted averages.

We then sent out the second-round Delphi questionnaire, which asked respondents to rank order the thirty-two elements and to provide comments. We received thirty-seven replies; the top ten elements were exactly the same as the top ten in the first round. We decided that a third round was not needed.

The Organizational Survey

With the help of a group of Virginia Tech HRD doctoral students, we then developed an organizational survey designed to collect data on:

1. The respondents' perception of "HRD effectiveness."
2. The respondents' opinion as to whether their HRD function was effective.
3. At least five examples of effectiveness.
4. Whether or not the respondents agreed with the list of critical elements (if they did use a particular element as a functional objective, they were asked to give an example).
5. Demographic variables (for example, size and type of organization, number of HRD staff).

We asked *Training Magazine* for a sample of the mailing list they use to conduct their annual survey. They provided us with 1,000 mailing labels supposedly representing organizations with 1,000 or more employees. (We wanted to be sure we reached organizations large enough to support an internal HRD function.) After carefully checking the labels, we ultimately mailed out 924 surveys. Three weeks later, after what seemed to us like a low response, we did a selected follow-up of 200 mailings. We received a final return of 14 percent (130 responses) which, although low when compared with returns for educational surveys, is average when compared with business surveys such as *Training Magazine* and the Conference Board studies of the HRD field. More important, our responses were representative of the various industrial classifications of organizations and of the major geographic areas of the country.

A little more than half of our respondents were employed in organizations of 1,000 to 10,000 people and one-quarter were in organizations of more than 10,000. The majority of these organizations had over six full-time HRD employees; roughly 15 percent have over thirty-seven. Our respondents did represent large organizations with well-staffed HRD functions, for the most part. Eighty-six percent of our respondents came from organizations with decentralized (as opposed to centralized) HRD functions. This is not surprising considering the cost of travel and the diversity of industry represented. While our conclusions may not be statistically generalizable, we believe they are descriptive of the state of HRD effectiveness in American organizations.

Our last activity was to contact the twenty-two respondents who agreed to be interviewed and who identified their HRD function as being effective. Ultimately we conducted sixteen interviews with, for the most part, directors of HRD/T&D functions of either major divisions of large corporations or of corporatewide units. We also reviewed every "training profile" article (starting from January 1983) in *Training Magazine,* as well as articles from the *Training Directors' Forum Newsletter* and *Training and Development Journal.* In addition, we solicited ideas and stories from our own professional networks and added anecdotes that we have collected from our combined thirty-plus years in the field. These interviews, articles, and stories gave us the examples of how effective HRD functions have been able to achieve their credibility and productivity. For those who would like more information about the research methodology, copies of each of the survey instruments, including the Delphi questionnaires and the organizational survey, are available from the authors upon request.

3

Critical Elements
of HRD Effectiveness:
Research Results

The world is round and the place which may seem
like the end may also be only the beginning.
——Ivy Baker Priest, Treasurer
of the United States, 1958

Our research took two years to complete, with hundreds of
hours of work by us and a group of Virginia Tech's HRD doctoral students, but we believe the results were worth the investment. The benefits we personally received from conducting the
research, from interacting with the HRD experts, from discussions with HRD practitioners, and from our readings were
invaluable. The results we obtained from the research provided
the foundation from which HRD practitioners can begin to
effectively provide the resources our organizations need.

Results of the Delphi Study

The Delphi phase of our research provided ten elements
that the panel of HRD experts considered essential to the success of an effective HRD function. There were no real surprises.
Future thinking was minimal; rather, the experts were solidly
grounded in past and immediate experience. The ten elements
that floated to the top of the critical list then could also be said
to be critical for any HRD unit at the present time, although
organizational type and culture might change the ranking. We

present the ten critical elements in rank order, with a discussion of the experts' comments.

1. The HRD Function Has the Expertise to Diagnose Problems in Order to Determine Appropriateness of Potential Solutions

This element surfaced as the single most critical set of actions needed for effective HRD functioning. That these are a *set* of actions was evidenced by the responses—a number of experts cited the need for the expertise, noting that it provides internal legitimacy to the HRD function, and an almost equal number addressed the need for problem diagnosis and solution identification. These were seen as givens within an effective HRD function, not goals. One respondent said, "The rest of HRD is paperwork. If this is a given, and not an accountability or a goal . . . everything else falls into place."

Another noted, "New technologies will place awesome demands on staff." Slides and tapes and classroom training have not been too difficult to identify and sort as potential solutions, they said, but "now we add in CAI, interactive video and tele-communications of all sorts, sizes and shapes, and the job gets tough!" Obtaining the expertise becomes significantly more difficult.

Analysis of the data finally forced us to break the responses under this critical event into three categories, all of which contribute to its significance:

1. Expertise to diagnose organizational problems.
2. Expertise to diagnose individual problems.
3. Expertise to identify solutions in terms of processes, products, and resources, and ultimately the expertise to recommend solutions.

After we had reviewed the comments and our analysis, several underlying assumptions became apparent to us.

1. Expertise acquisition must be available—which means that HRD practitioners must identify what they need to become "expert": they must understand the tasks, knowledge, and

skills required of them and the standards for "expert" behavior. The American Society for Training and Development's 1983 competence study, "Models for Excellence," is one source of information for the HRD side of the job; we will discuss the need for industry knowledge later.

2. Access must be given to data necessary for problem diagnosis. The HRD function must be allowed to reach into the guts of the organization; the function must be *trusted*.
3. The HRD function also needs to have enough leverage and visibility in the organization to be able to collect the data. The organization as a whole must be willing to allow the data collection to take place—the *trust* element again.
4. The HRD function needs to have the credibility to make recommendations on potential solutions. This implies a track record, and so we have a potential chicken and egg situation building. How do you develop a track record without credibility? (See a brief discussion of this dilemma at the end of the next chapter.)

2. The HRD Manager Maintains an Active Network with Other Key Managers in the Organization

One respondent quipped, "You gotta have friends." Positioning this as the second most important contribution to effectiveness indicated that people recognize that more important information frequently resides in the informal networks within an organization than in any formal management information system.

This element was perceived as part of the necessary process of understanding the organizational culture: its values, its personality, and its myths. With this understanding, the HRD manager can identify and deal with hidden agendas, and does not become powerless in political infighting. The manager of an effective HRD function *knows* who is "in" and who is on the way out, is privy to the newest strategic directions, and does not allow the HRD function to become vulnerable to strategy and policy changes. The effective HRD manager is seldom surprised at what happens in the organization!

The underlying assumptions here are

1. The HRD manager is high enough in the organization or has enough networking skill to establish the necessary linkages.
2. There is a tradeoff. There have to be payoffs for other managers to share information with the HRD manager: perceived or real power, information, needed resources—friendship.

3. There Is a Corporate Training and Development Mission Statement or Corporate HRD Policy

This, the third-ranked element, was seen as an essential framework for the HRD function. Our respondents said that the mission statement or policies do not necessarily need to be overtly stated. They might exist in the form of an operating plan and budget; they might also be implied in the culture of the organization. Xerox does not have a single corporationwide published mission statement with regard to HRD, but the existence of a multimillion-dollar Xerox Training Center in Leesburg, Virginia, makes a clear statement about HRD policy in the corporation.

Two underlying assumptions:

1. Mission statements are *used* in the organization to give direction to action; they are not merely "window dressing."
2. The corporate culture is visible; hidden agendas do not dominate the culture.

4. The Evaluation of Training Focuses on Behavioral Change or Organizational Results

Formal evaluation of training in an effective HRD function takes place in some form, but *not* the "smile sheets" or "happiness measures" still used by many trainers at the end of a training session. The effective HRD function generally uses competency-based training and evaluates against clearly stated course outcomes for accountability reasons: to find out if behaviors have indeed changed as stated in the course objectives, or if the course needs to be revised in some way, or to make decisions about HRD interventions.

On-the-job performance is more important to these types of HRD functions than rave reviews at the end of a session. We do not discount rave reviews; they are very important for the HRD function's credibility. However, if the desired behaviors and competencies stated in the course objectives are seen in evidence by supervisors, peers, and subordinates when the trainee returns to the job, many of our respondents noted that the rave reviews will be there.

In effective HRD organizations, decisions to conduct a course a second time, change it, or stop its presentation are based to a great extent on the results of the evaluations conducted.

The underlying assumptions:

1. The course has been developed as a result of a valid front-end analysis (the need was initially established and validated), and evidence of need for the course is frequently updated. When this is the case, evaluation of training becomes a matter of determining whether or not the desired competencies were achieved, to what level, and if not, why not.
2. There exists within the organization the professional knowledge and skill to perform not only front-end analyses, but evaluations.
3. Front-end analysis and evaluation standards exist and are communicated throughout the HRD function.

5. The HRD Manager Routinely Participates in Corporate Strategy Sessions with Other Key Staff Persons and Senior Managers

Many of our panel respondents indicated that they did routinely participate in corporate strategy and planning sessions. The fairly high fifth-place ranking of this element indicated to us that many of our panel members were themselves high up in their organizations and see the corporate planning session as a normal part of their everyday life. Several noted that they had negotiated their inclusion in this level of planning as a part of their agreement to take their current positions.

For many HRD managers, this may translate into having input into the annual operating plan at an early enough stage to make some impact. It may mean being included in the early stages of discussion of a new product. In a large number of responses, it was seen as a desirable but not yet fully achieved objective.

The underlying assumptions:

1. The HRD manager is high enough in the corporate or organizational superstructure to take part in this level of discussion.
2. The effective HRD function is an integral part of the strategic and developmental thinking processes of the organization of which it is a part.
3. Effective HRD functions are viewed as valuable to their organizations, and for good reasons. Their managers operate at fairly high levels of management, and they produce!

6. Training Needs Associated with Major Changes in the Organization Are Anticipated

In this scenario, as in element 5 above, the HRD function is viewed as an asset, not a liability, according to the panelists. This critical element is actually linked directly to element 5: our Delphi panel said that if the HRD manager is a part of the strategic thinking and planning processes of the organization, then she will be a part of the change design process and will be able to identify and plan for the required training at the same time. In an effective HRD function, they said, the HRD manager is involved in all levels of organizational planning.

Sometimes the major change itself requires training as the primary means of implementation. When Xerox identified a need to change the corporate culture for survival of the corporation, the vehicle chosen to communicate the need and the methods for turning the company around was an extensive internal training process.

The underlying assumptions:

1. When new technology is introduced into an organization, the HRD function's involvement in the change process can be a reflection of its perceived effectiveness.
2. The organization (of which the HRD function is a part) assumes that training will take place as the organization changes—and the organization knows that change is inevitable.

7. Allocations of HRD Resources Are Based at Least in Part on the Priorities of the Organization

Our panelists indicated that an effective HRD function develops a one-, two-, or five-year operating plan that is directly linked to the organization's defined priorities, at least in part. Several of our panel members felt strongly that the effective HRD function must also engage in future thinking and planning, and certainly a part of its resources must be targeted in some way to meeting the HRD needs of the organization five to ten years out as well as within the current fiscal year.

The underlying assumptions:

1. The organization's priorities are clearly defined.
2. The HRD function has had the priorities communicated to it, understands them, and understands its role and responsibilities in relation to the priorities.

8. The HRD Function Conducts Needs Assessments to Determine Organizational Requirements

The Delphi panelists noted that the effective HRD function, when directly involved in all organizational planning, is normally called on to conduct various types of front-end analyses (task analysis, needs assessments), performance analysis, or organizational diagnosis to determine when training or other interventions may be required to improve productivity, the quality of work life, or organizational functioning.

The underlying assumptions:

1. The expertise exists in the effective HRD function to conduct front-end analyses.
2. The organization will allow needs assessments and task analyses to take place; the HRD function has the credibility to move into its organization whenever front-end analysis is required, and line personnel will contribute whatever time and effort it takes for HRD personnel to collect the necessary data.

9. The Roles, Responsibilities, and Priorities of the HRD Function Are Clearly Defined

The respondents indicated that in the effective HRD function, these ingredients are not only clearly defined, but they also are consistent with the roles and responsibilities of staff in the rest of the organization. But—and this was a big "but" from several of our panelists—they are not set in concrete. This flexibility sets a model for the larger organization.

Our panelists went on to say that in the effective HRD function, roles and responsibilities are not only clearly defined by those people performing the tasks, but the titles and compensation make sense. People are not elevated into management positions because they have been with the company for twenty years, and now it is time to reward "good old Sam" by giving him the HRD function. In organizations where this occurs, the assumption exists in upper management that a good sales manager will make a good HRD manager, and while this may be true in some cases, frequently it is disastrous for the HRD function.

We were clearly told that the most effective HRD functions are managed and staffed by professional HRD personnel who also know their industry or business. When this situation exists, they are able to build and model appropriate HRD performance with their staff in appropriate roles.

The underlying assumptions:

1. Organizations recognize the value of hiring and training HRD professionals to manage the HRD function.

2. Organizations recognize the value of ensuring professional
    HRD training and education for line personnel moving into
    the HRD function.

10. The HRD Management and Staff Routinely Meet to Discuss Problems and Progress with Current Programs

Our panel told us that in the effective HRD function,
clear and open communications are built into the function's
operating model. There is a high level of trust. The managers
are trusted because they communicate openly with staff, and
they trust their personnel to produce what is required of them.

There is a great deal of participation in the management
of the function by all levels, but the managers do not ask their
staff to perform tasks that they (the managers) would not be
willing to do themselves. People know that it is OK to make
honest mistakes, that they will not be punished. Because of this
openness, problems surface early when they can be dealt with
more easily.

Another point the panelists made was that various meeting styles and formats are used to accommodate a variety of
thinking and communicating preferences. People at all levels
seem to have fun; they don't take themselves too seriously. Management and staff genuinely enjoy each other's company; meetings are usually fun and not punishing. They also noted that
paperwork is kept to a minimum: people are rewarded for communicating verbally or electronically and not distributing unnec-
essary paper. Idea generation and creativity are rewarded.

The underlying assumptions:

1. Idea generation and creativity are considered by the organi-
    zation as well as the HRD function to be essential to prob-
    lem solving.
2. Behaviors that build trust are valued and rewarded by the
    organization; behaviors that endanger trust are not rewarded.

The HRD Effectiveness Survey

Our original objective in conducting this survey was to
validate the results of the Delphi study by asking HRD managers

if they agreed with the HRD experts. But the essence of research is to try to collect data as objectively as possible; so instead of asking managers outright if they agreed or disagreed with "the experts" (which they might answer based on how they feel about experts rather than how they feel about the issues), we started out by asking totally different questions.

First we needed practitioners to define *effectiveness*. We could not ask them about their HRD effectiveness unless we knew what their specific operational definitions were. So we asked how they would describe an effective HRD function (see Figure 1).

Our only surprise was the low response to the item about budget constraints. Perhaps few HRD managers feel that having or controlling financial resources is critical to being effective. Or possibly those that responded to our questionnaire do have this control; thus it is for them a given, a condition that simply goes with the territory of effective HRD management. Figure 1 also presents several descriptors that the respondents added. One of them is "good use of resources"; using resources wisely seemed to be much more critical than having an abundance of resources. It is simply a matter of good business practice.

Figure 1. Definition of HRD Effectiveness.

How would you describe an effective HRD function?

1. Function perceived by organization as asset.	90%
2. Top management perceives and uses function as critical resource.	89%
3. High level of internal and external trust.	85%
4. Function placed at appropriate level in organization.	84%
5. High level of creativity encouraged; staff enjoys working in the function.	79%
6. No (or few) budget constraints.	15%

Additional Descriptors

1. Function meets customer needs, individual and organizational.
2. Good use of all resources.
3. The HRD function is integrated with overall corporate strategy.
4. HRD managers are part of or connected to senior staff.

We then asked a very simple but significant question: "Do you consider your HRD function to be effective?" Responses: 64.5% said yes, 14.5% no, and 21% were uncertain. One caution: it was not our intent to determine *how many* HRD functions are effective, but to have respondents declare their perceptions so that we could focus on *how* they achieved their effectiveness. We wanted to study the effective functions, not the ineffective ones. It is quite possible that some managers who perceived their functions as ineffective did not respond to our survey. It would be wrong to conclude that two-thirds of *all* HRD functions perceive themselves as being effective.

The next question was probably the most critical. We asked those managers who perceived their functions as being effective to list five actions or activities that contributed to their success. Figure 2 represents a content analysis of all the statements they listed; actual examples of the statements can be found in Chapters Five, Six, and Seven.

Figure 2. Actions That Contribute to HRD Effectiveness.

1. The HRD function is perceived as a *responsive* resource (as responsible, not reactive).
2. There is close communication and a close working relationship with line and staff management.
3. The function is supported by highly professional staff.
4. The function is perceived as having a successful track record.

1. The HRD Function Is Perceived as a Responsive Resource

Survey statements mentioned concepts such as:

The HRD function is perceived as (internal) consultants/ counselors and mentors.
The HRD function supports the organization's goals and objectives.
Training is viewed as part of the business.
The HRD function supports organizational change.

The key idea that jumped out at us was that effective HRD functions are responsive to the needs of their customers (the larger organization they serve) in a responsible, professional sense rather than a reactive, "fighting fires" sense.

2. There Is Close Communication and a Close Working Relationship with Line and Staff Management

Survey statements such as these supported the theme of strong internal networking.

> Good communications in the organization.
> Relationships with individual managers.
> HRD works with managers on their level.
> HRD works on strategic planning teams.

3. The Function Is Supported by Highly Professional Staff

This was a particularly surprising finding, considering that professional development of HRD specialists has not been a hot topic at national conferences, nor has it been particularly emphasized in the professional literature. Items under this heading included:

> Strong sense of teamwork.
> Emphasis on training and development for HRD staff.
> Highly ethical (professional) conduct (performance) valued.
> Evaluation to improve, not prove.
> High level of creativity and flexibility.

The message that came through loud and clear was that a highly professional, well-trained, experienced HRD team is essential to the success of the function.

4. The Function Is Perceived as Having a Successful Track Record

Effective HRD functions painstakingly built a history of results-oriented activities. This category included statements such as:

Quality development of programs.
A systems approach to training.
Good marketing and cost control.
Reality-based systems.

Track records like these are not established with one dynamite program. Constant attention to details and deliberately building credibility were emphasized over and over again. (Note that many of the comments actually fit into more than one category, depending on their interpretation.)

We then asked the respondents a series of questions that were actually the ten critical elements in partial disguise. We wanted them to tell us whether they actually applied the elements in their organizations and if so, to cite an example for each (see Figure 3). All ten statements were confirmed by more than half the respondents, except for one: the statement on whether they did needs analysis designed to identify anticipated organizational changes.

The questions on top management involvement, clearly delineated roles and responsibilities, and participation in strategy sessions all had a weak majority confirmation. Yet the lowest confirmation was still 47 percent, a significant measure. This section of our survey told us that those items the Delphi experts identified as critical were actually pieces of a larger picture. The next chapter describes our struggle to organize these findings in a way that would reveal that larger picture.

Figure 3. Critical Elements in Action.

Question	Yes	No	Uncertain
1. Does the manager of your HRD function have regular contact with other key managers in the organization?	79%	8%	12%
2. Does the HRD staff (including the HRD manager) meet regularly to discuss problems and review progress of projects?	73%	12%	15%
3. Does your HRD function have the *expertise* to determine and implement appropriate solutions once problems are diagnosed?	72%	11%	17%

Figure 3. Critical Elements in Action, Cont'd.

Question	Yes	No	Uncertain
4. Does training evaluation in your organization focus either on behavioral change or organization results or both?	72%	9%	19%
5. Do you allocate resources of the HRD function based on the priorities of the organization?	72%	12%	16%
6. Does your HRD function have the expertise to diagnose organizational problems?	67%	16%	16%
7. Does your organization have a formal corporate training and development mission statement and/or corporate HRD policies?	65%	23%	11%
8. Do you periodically review and/or revise your organization's formal training and development mission statement and/or corporate HRD policies?	60%	26%	16%
9. Do you have a top management group or collection of top managers that involve themselves in the policies and activities of the HRD function?	58%	29%	13%
10. Do you or your HRD manager participate in corporate strategy sessions with key staff persons and senior managers?	54%	32%	16%
11. Are the roles, responsibilities, and priorities of the HRD function clearly defined?	52%	31%	19%
12. Is your training needs analysis designed to identify anticipated organizational changes? (Is your system future-oriented rather than crisis-oriented?)	47%	38%	14%

4

The HRD Effectiveness Model

A vision articulates a view of a realistic, credible, attractive future for the organization, a condition that is better in some important ways than what now exists . . . a vision is a target that beckons.
> ——Warren Bennis and
> Burt Nanus,
> *Leaders,* 1985

One of the criticisms of HRD research often heard in our field is that research findings and conclusions are presented in ways that are not really useful to practitioners. One of the criticisms often heard about practitioners is that they are looking for instant tools and fast answers to make their jobs easier. Since we feel both criticisms are often valid, we wanted to take what we hope is a balanced approach and present our findings in a way that is consistent with the purpose of this book, which is to provide a practical and useful tool developed from the research findings: the HRD Effectiveness Model. It combines the findings from the Delphi study and the organization survey in a framework that will help you evaluate your own HRD function.

As we began to develop a useful model from the research findings, the first question we faced was whether the results of the organization survey validated the results of the Delphi study. Did the practitioners agree with the experts? Our conclusion was a resounding "yes and no." A majority of respondents (except in one case, where the response was a significant minority of 47 percent) validated the ten Delphi elements. While we perceived the ten elements as the end product, the organization survey respondents saw them as a means to an end. Their "end"

30

became the four major conclusions: responsive resource, close relationships, highly professional staff, and track record.

We started to build our model from this premise—four goals and numerous objectives (the ten Delphi elements plus the groups of survey statements from which the four goals were derived). But when we tried to cluster the objectives under the four goals, there was too much overlap. The more we tried to force fit the objectives with the goals, the more frustrated we became. Finally, we stepped back and discussed what we were trying to achieve. We reminded ourselves that we wanted to use the findings to help HRD functions evaluate their performance. When we acknowledged this, we were able to conclude that we needed to use a performance-oriented framework. We then identified the overriding *goal* of the effective HRD function:

Goal
Build a Responsive Resource

We saw this goal as capturing the essence of all the findings. It evoked a vision of a thoroughly competent, professional HRD team constantly building and maintaining a track record of high-quality products and services through close relationships with line and staff management and now enjoying (in all senses of that word) the credibility it deserves. This is our vision of what HRD effectiveness is all about.

The foundation for this vision is the three criteria that must be achieved to make the vision reality:

Criteria
1. A highly professional HRD staff.
2. Close relationships with line and staff management.
3. A track record of high-quality products and services.

The way to achieve these criteria and fulfill the vision is to meet the following standards:

Standards

1. The HRD function has ability to diagnose problems and anticipate needs.
2. The HRD function is supported by a corporate HRD mission statement or organizational culture.
3. The HRD function has a commitment to strategic planning and supporting organizational change.
4. The roles and responsibilities of the HRD staff are clearly defined.
5. The HRD function has a commitment to front-end analysis and evaluation.
6. The function has a strong commitment to its own staff development.
7. The HRD function is perceived as an internal consultant to management.
8. The HRD function has a strong marketing and public relations capability.
9. The members of the HRD staff are perceived as experts.
10. There is a high level of HRD staff teamwork, creativity, and flexibility.
11. There is a high level of ethical conduct by the HRD staff.
12. The HRD function is perceived as "part of the business."
13. There is a high level of congruence between HRD function and organizational goals and objectives.
14. The HRD function is perceived as conducting reality-based programs.
15. There is a high level of networking for all levels of management.

We found that all the standards apply to some extent to each of the three criteria. We structured the model as a matrix based on this conclusion and developed questions for each box in the matrix (see Figure 4). With this format, you can choose the questions that are appropriate for your organization and then develop answers that meet your needs.

The matrix is a guide to help you accomplish what is required to build, develop, or establish an effective HRD function. The next three chapters will give you insight into how others have actually accomplished some of these standards—you don't have to start from scratch.

Before we move on, though, we want you to think about one underlying dilemma: what comes first—HRD credibility or top management support? It is a classic chicken and egg dilemma, one for which we found no easy answers. What we did find is the logical answer: if you do not have top management support, you are going to have to build your credibility to get it. If you do have top management support, great! But you are still going to have to prove yourself and ensure that your credibility meets management's expectations. Either way, achieving effectiveness is hard work. Please consider this as you read the next three chapters.

Figure 4. HRD Effectiveness Model.

Goal: Building a Responsive Resource

Standards	Criteria		
	Close relationship with line and staff management	*Highly professional HRD staff*	*Track record of high-quality products and services*
1. HRD function has ability to diagnose problems and anticipate needs.	What are methods for gaining the close relationship that will allow access to organizational data? How can trust be achieved to allow the HRD function into the larger organization to collect necessary data?	What kind of expertise is needed? (For example, ability to diagnose organizational and individual problems and recommend appropriate solutions.) How is needed competence achieved?	How can HRD functions make recommendations and deliver appropriate solutions to diagnosed problems? What is at stake when needs are diagnosed correctly, but are not what the organization wants to hear?
2. HRD function is supported by corporate HRD mission statement or organizational culture.	How can HRD function ensure that its mission statement and an understanding of HRD purpose are clearly understood at all levels and across all subunits of the organization?	How can HRD professional staff facilitate the development of an HRD mission statement? Can the HRD staff influence organizational culture?	What needs to be done to ensure that HRD function's output is congruent with mission statement? Are some public relations efforts better than others?
3. HRD function has commitment to strategic planning and supporting organizational change.	How can HRD staff first get involved in strategic planning? What can they do to stay involved?	How can professional staff be better prepared to support strategic planning and organizational change?	What can HRD staff produce to demonstrate commitment to strategic planning and organizational change?

4. Roles and responsibilities of the HRD staff are clearly defined.	How can HRD staff best model the role and responsibility definition process for the larger organization?	What techniques and resources are available to facilitate this process?	What are some of the ways to demonstrate payoff of clear role and responsibility definition to the larger organization?
5. HRD function has commitment to front-end analysis (FEA) and evaluation.	How can line and staff management be involved in front-end analysis? How can they be involved in ongoing evaluations?	What specific competencies and skills are required in today's organizations to conduct front-end analyses and evaluations? How can the HRD function develop these skills and competencies in staff? Are valid instructional design principles and processes used and understood by all personnel?	How can time spent in FEA and evaluation be depicted to the larger organization as producing a valid return on time invested in the effort? Can the HRD function correlate a financial return on investment to FEA? To evaluation?
6. Function has strong commitment to HRD staff development.	What role does management play in HRD staff development? Is staff development integrated into performance evaluations? If it is, how is this done?	Do effective HRD functions "make" or "buy" professionalism? How is staff development managed for maximum efficiency and effectiveness? How are personal and organizational goals aligned in effective HRD organizations?	How can HRD function show direct connection between professional products developed by staff and ongoing professional development?

Figure 4. HRD Effectiveness Model, Cont'd.

Goal: Building a Responsive Resource

Standards	Criteria		
	Close relationship with line and staff management	*Highly professional HRD staff*	*Track record of high-quality products and services*
7. HRD function is perceived as internal consultant to management.	What kinds of legitimate "networking" activities can HRD staff perform with line and staff management to institutionalize the function as viable internal consultants?	What types of professional development activities prepare HRD staff to function as internal consultants to management? How can the internal consulting capability best be communicated to management?	How can the HRD function capitalize on its track records to establish itself as an internal consultant?
8. Function has a strong marketing and public relations capability.	Should the HRD function market to line and staff management?	Are there ethical limits to marketing professional staff? How can marketing and PR capabilities be developed?	Is a track record dependent on PR? Can an HRD function establish a track record without marketing and PR activities? If so, how can this be done?
9. Members of the HRD staff are perceived as experts.	What role does the relationship between the HRD function and line and staff management play in the organization's perception of the HRD function as expert?	Can this be done without a highly professional staff?	Can a track record be established if the HRD function is *not* perceived as a group of experts by the larger organization?

10. There is a high level of HRD staff teamwork, creativity, and flexibility.	Can teamwork, creativity, and flexibility occur in HRD functions when these elements are not present in the larger organization? How can close HRD function relationships with line and staff management help line and staff to be more creative and flexible?	Are creativity, teamwork, and flexibility a result of professionalism? Do effective HRD functions spend time developing teamwork, creativity, and flexibility?	Do factors such as teamwork, creativity, and flexibility contribute to high-quality products and services in effective HRD organizations?
11. There is a high level of HRD staff ethical conduct.	Where should HRD staff loyalties lie—to the profession or the organization?	Is there a relationship between professionalism and ethical conduct; is either necessary to the other?	Is it possible to produce high-quality products and services *without* a high level of ethical conduct?
12. The HRD function is perceived as "part of the business."	What is the balance in effective HRD functions between being perceived by line and staff as professional, and being perceived by staff as "field relevant" or "part of the business"?	What types of professional development activities for HRD staff are required to ensure that the function is perceived as "part of the business"?	In effective HRD functions, how are quality products and services best produced as "part of the business"?
13. There is a high level of congruence between HRD function and organizational goals and objectives.	Is the congruence a direct result of the close relationship of line and staff management to the HRD function?	In effective HRD functions, is the congruence a direct result of HRD professional development?	What is the relationship between congruence and high-quality products and services?

Figure 4. HRD Effectiveness Model, Cont'd.

Goal: Building a Responsive Resource

Standards	Close relationship with line and staff management	Highly professional HRD staff	Track record of high-quality products and services
		Criteria	
14. The function is perceived as conducting reality-based programs.	What is the relationship between the function being perceived as conducting reality-based programs and the degree of HRD functional relationship with line and staff management?	Is this dependent on an HRD professional staff, or can reality-based programs be bought "off the shelf"?	Can a track record be established with anything other than reality-based programs?
15. There is a high level of networking with all levels of management.	How can a new HRD function develop these "network relationships"?	Do professional practitioners network more easily with other professionals than with management?	How does "networking with all levels of management" contribute to the production of high-quality products and services?

5

Xc——————————————————————————•••X

Close Relationships
with Management

We are all, it seems, saving ourselves for the senior
prom. But many of us forget that somewhere along
the way we must learn to dance.
———Alan Harrington,
Life in the Crystal Palace,
1939

Not surprisingly, our research identified the need for building
and maintaining close relationships with line and staff management as essential for a successful HRD organization. The questions that arise from this requirement have to do with *size and
process:* how do you get invited to the prom in the first place,
and how close should you dance? What can you do if you don't
get an invitation to the party, and if you do, what is the most
appropriate behavior to get asked back?

Depending on the size and culture of your organization,
this can be a relatively simple task, this business of developing
close management relationships, or an almost impossible one.
Given a small organization, with less than 2,000 or 3,000
employees, and a fairly centralized location with an open culture, the essential close relationships are easy enough to build.

Change any one of these factors (increase organizational
size, decentralize operations, or create a hierarchical, formalized
corporate culture), and the task of building close relationships
becomes far more difficult.

In this chapter we look first at "how close is close," then
report on how and why managers of successful HRD organiza-

tions take the time and expend the effort to build these relationships. Finally, we will address the questions posed in the HRD Effectiveness Model.

How Close Is Close?

This really does depend on your organization and your communication processes. At one extreme, if you, as a manager of an HRD function, never see senior management, are not involved in any type of strategic planning, or never even get into the field, then you are indeed isolated from both the formal and informal communication networks of your organization. You can begin by using any one of the several techniques we discuss below. For you, "close" may mean (at least for a while) sharing information on your own function with your larger organization, and doing this systematically and regularly.

If, on the other end of the continuum, you meet regularly with senior staff, take part in all organizational strategic planning and have lunch regularly with the chief executive officer, "close" for you means the phone call from the CEO asking for your advice on a potential merger and its impact on human resource development in the total organization.

Most HRD managers are somewhere between these two extremes, working for clearer two-way communications on everyone's part—because that means the HRD function can be more effective in meeting the needs of the larger organization. If that level of communication is what HRD functions are striving for, how are they doing it?

When You Need to Connect, Set Up a Task Force. It really does work! Gail George at Perpetual American Bank told us that in her organization the HRD function works closely with two main training-related task groups. One specifically deals with the management trainees in such areas as selection criteria, interviews, and needs analysis. The second task group, which deals with the more experienced managers, has responsibility for topics related to management development.

We studied an eighty-five–person HRD department that serves the sales and marketing division of a high-tech organization with more than 100,000 employees overall. This HRD department provides a variety of high-quality training services through extensive use of front-end analyses, needs analyses, and intensive involvement of subject matter experts from the field. Recently a new unit was established in this organization to provide computer assisted instruction (CAI), which could potentially serve any of the multiple units within the HRD function. Although senior staff had been aware of a need for some type of curriculum coordinating committee, it was the new CAI unit's need for input from all levels of line and staff management to help identify and rank candidates for CAI that galvanized the HRD function into taking action. Without a committee of training *and* field personnel given the specific responsibility for saying that these are appropriate candidates for CAI and these are the field priorities, the CAI unit was isolated by geography and company culture from line and staff. Without the connection provided by the coordinating committee, the CAI unit was in the position of selling services but not necessarily meeting customer needs—they were dancing alone!

Identify with Top Management Goals. Several study respondents indicated that although they wanted management involvement in HRD policy development, it was hard to come by. One interviewee said, "It's really a matter of priorities. They just don't have time. The informal relationship is very good, though."

Robert Desatnick, former corporate vice president for personnel for McDonald's Corporation, succinctly identified the HRD function's need to identify with top management goals as an "acid test for effectiveness" when he wrote: "Successful human resource functions periodically survey their internal clients (senior management) to determine the relevance, importance, and contribution of their discipline to management objectives and goals. Their approach is similar to the marketing executive who continually measures consumer reaction to the company's products" (1984).

Before introducing new policies, projects, or programs, credible human resource executives determine in advance the

degree to which they meet client needs. According to Desatnick
(p. 44), they ask these questions:

> How useful is the management structure?
> Is it in usable form?
> Will it actually be used to solve problems, or will it be
> circumvented?

Desatnick describes the human resource director in a diver-
sified food processing company who asked his senior managers
to rank four major proposed personnel projects. Because of
budget and staffing constraints, only one project could be
launched. The managers were asked to determine which project,
from their perspective, would most favorably affect business
results. The project eventually selected involved a study of corporate staff positions to identify how each contributed to business results. It seems that the corporate office had grown out of
proportion to increases in sales and profits (a problem all too
common these days). The project concluded with the elimination
of a significant number of positions, which shortened lines of
communication and improved efficiency. Desatnick notes that
recommendations were put in usable form for implementation
and were used by senior management to reverse an unhealthy
situation.

Imagine, if you can, how far such a proposed action
would have gotten had it not come from a team of senior
management, but rather from the HRD function directly—even
though the rationale and recommendations might have been
similar to the team's proposed project. Imagine, too, how
much richer and more reality-driven the product of such a
team effort must be than recommendations from HRD function
input alone. This is not to say that HRD personnel do not
have valid contributions to this type of decision-making process. However, hard decisions are best made in concert with
those people who will be affected by them. In the case of the
HRD function in most organizations, this means management
at all levels.

Desatnick summed up this issue when he wrote:

Human resource executives who fail often busy
themselves with a myriad of details. They fail to
delegate and in spreading themselves too thin, they
over-commit and so produce slipshod work. They
seldom reflect on how to measure and improve their
business contribution. They position themselves as
ombudspersons and advocates for the masses of
employees. In so doing, they fail to identify with
top management goals. They add to the burden
by attempting to do the line manager's job in solving people problems. Unsuccessful human resource
practitioners do not respond adequately to top management concerns . . . they fail to anticipate, and
then react . . . they tend to have too many objectives, and too few of those are relevant to business.
They arrive early and stay late. They make emo-
tional appeals for additional staff and budget as
opposed to presenting cold, hard facts and precise
position papers. As their burden multiplies, they
overlook important details such as returning phone
calls and responding to requests from line managers
for assistance [p. 46].

In other words, they isolate themselves from management—a
certain guarantee for the failure of an HRD function.

However, knowing management goals is only one part of
this essential criteria. The successful HRD function acts on
them, and feeds that information back to management.

Let Top Management Know What You're Doing. We
might also call this technique "dancing to the same tune."
According to Geri Kurlander, associate director of personnel,
planning, and development for the industrial products group
of Union Carbide, people in the training business need to go
to management and make a clear case about what they can
deliver. Top managers, she notes, must be aware and confident
that the HRD function can be used as a wedge to get at
unsettled problems.

Kurlander was involved in the final stage of a two-year turnaround of a strategically important plant and pipeline complex in the southwestern United States. "Some problems stemmed from a poor technical management structure, a crisis-oriented management style and a hostile labor environment with regard to any type of change" (1986, p. 4). First she assembled a study team of six management and production personnel who could help identify and analyze specific problems. She identified the key players (the labor relations manager, the local plant manager, the employee relations representative at the plant, a key production supervisor, the director of production for the entire operation, and the regional production director) and brought them together to determine what could be done and what each of their roles would be.

Next, a team of three, including a technical expert from another plant who had no ax to grind with the southwestern operation, conducted a three-day, on-site needs analysis, which included a structured interview process. A full, in-depth understanding of the plant could not be established in that short time, Kurlander said, but enough data was gathered to determine the major issues and identify the patterns of the facility.

After two years of analysis and implementation, the company has been better able to address performance issues. Management now consistently acknowledges that job performance matters, and that Kurlander's function can do something about it. Kurlander says, "Remember that successful internal management development is market driven. Take your clients where they are at—if a client tells you he has a broken window, don't tell him about his leaky roof. Fix the window first and you can go back and talk later about the roof" (p. 4).

Take "management development" out of the sentence above and replace it with "human resource development." Then note that, as many of our respondents said, you not only must be in line with management goals, but you must connect with management to find out what the goals are, and then let management know that you are working toward them.

Charlie Fields, at Hartford Steam Boiler says, "My mission is to help people think better." He has laid the groundwork through his formal training programs, but he also writes articles for company publications and trade journals, and circulates to managers other items he finds that support what he is trying to accomplish. "I use the *Wall Street Journal, Forbes,* and other publications the managers recognize in order to sell the ideas. I stay with some trendy stuff and tag onto it—like an amendment to legislation" ("Profile: Charles Fields," 1986, p. 6).

A number of training managers say that they share business information up and down, good and bad. Plant managers are invited to HRD meetings to talk about the state of their part of the business, top management is invited to brief the HRD function on the overall state of the business, and HRD personnel are encouraged to communicate upward with ideas and comments.

To quote Robert Desatnick once more: "It is incumbent on human resource practitioners to teach others in the organization the effective use of their discipline and to demonstrate its importance. CEOs expect that the assets they allocate to the human resource function will bring a return fully commensurate with increases in human resources staffing and compensation. High visibility brings with it a challenge; it alone will not bring success. It merely provides the opportunity to succeed—or, conversely, the chance to fail" (1984, p. 46).

Get Involved in the Strategic Planning Process. "Sure," you say, "that's easy enough to write about, but it can really be difficult to do." True, but our study respondents told us that where the HRD function is actively involved in the organization's strategic planning process, the relationships with line and staff management necessary for a successful HRD function usually are developed.

At New England Telephone, strategic planning is a formal process in the company, and the HRD function is an active participant. Marty Smith told us that they produce a yearly document, but the end product is much more than the strategic planning document: there is real consensus resulting from the planning process. Smith says their planning meetings are based on the department head's belief that planning facilitates a shared set of beliefs about the future that resides in people's heads; in meetings shared with line and staff, key ideas are distilled and consensus building creates a theme for the total organization.

In organizations that are market- or product-driven, the HRD function that is *not* included in the strategic planning process can find itself in the unnatural and uncomfortable position of (1) not being able to anticipate its customers' needs and (2) frequently not being able to meet those needs. This condition can be significantly accelerated by economic or market changes. Not having HRD involved in the strategic planning process also denies the organization the particular training and development perspective that HRD brings to the party.

How do you make this happen? One HRD manager we know was actually responsible for starting the strategic planning process in her organization. Another documented the effect of his *not* being included by identifying the person-hours spent in reactive "knee-jerk" problem solving that would have been avoided had he been involved in the strategic planning process in the first place. Another HRD manager developed a strategic plan for her own function, then invited the senior staff to a meeting where she presented the plan and showed how it supported the larger organization's mission statement. She was invited to the next strategic planning meeting of her larger organization! If you are not involved in the strategic planning processes of your organization, identify its mission and goals, and start with your own strategic plan, then distribute it to appropriate levels of management for input. At least you will get the music started.

Three other obvious, but sometimes difficult, activities are useful in building and maintaining these essential relationships: talking to other trainers, listening to everyone in your organization, and using line and staff managers as subject matter experts.

Talk to Trainers. Ed Robbins, training director at Gelco Corporation, a $1 billion Minnesota-based auto leasing business with 7,000 employees and 560 offices worldwide, says: "We've positioned ourselves to provide program leadership and to encourage other divisions to share information. Each division has its own missions, but I've worked to keep communications open—calling other trainers and being available when they need help."

In a large organization, talking only to other trainers within your own function has some danger if you do not also talk to trainers in *other* organizations. HRD people are not immune to "group think" or the Watergate Syndrome. Ideas that seem totally plausible within one organization may have been tried in a different environment with disastrous results.

Make Yourself Available to Listen. This may well be one of the most critical activities for building and maintaining close relationships with line and staff management. To put it another way, dancing cheek to cheek is not much fun with someone who is not listening as you whisper into his ear—or, even worse, is talking while you are trying to say something you think is really important. You will not want to dance with that person again!

Russell Young, vice president of training for Lomas and Nettleton, a Dallas-based mortgage banking firm, estimates he spends 80 percent of his work day planning and talking with his staff, line managers, and senior management, listening for problems, and discussing solutions to help the company cope with growth and change.

Young, who has been with the company for thirteen years, says, "The company is making lots of acquisitions. Understandably, that is the main focus now and part of why training has been somewhat slow" ("Profile: Russell Young," 1986, p. 6). Young says his frank criticism of the company's training deficiencies helped earn him a spot on the human resources advisory committee and his responsibility for developing the training department. He says, "Listening has been my saving grace in running a successful department. I am listening more now than I ever have in my life. And I think that is what helps keep training properly focused . . . there is so much going on in our organization and our industry that my job is not very hard. I just listen."

Use Line and Staff Managers. Effective HRD functions do not take chances when it comes to building the necessary relationships. In one way or another they involve employees of the larger organization—from the president or CEO on down—in seminars, presentations, surveys, and training sessions, building cooperation and credibility.

One very successful HRD function uses line and staff managers as subject matter experts in a variety of ways: on advisory boards and curriculum development and review committees, to review curriculum materials in all stages of development, in task and needs analyses. This organization never fails to feed back in some format the results of the managers' input with notes of thanks. Various members of the HRD organization have spent time in the field with line and staff managers and consequently know them well enough to call a well-informed internal network whenever facts need to be reviewed or information sought or verified.

The bottom line is the simple fact that effective HRD organizations are *connected* to the larger organization they serve in a variety of ways, both formal and informal. Some they have to initiate, others are part of the culture of the larger organization. They stay in step with the larger organization when the tempo changes—even if they are not always dancing cheek to cheek.

Maintaining Close Relationships—The Model

Let us now move to the HRD Effectiveness Model. You will recall that one criterion essential for effectiveness is "close relationships with line and staff management." You may also recall that we applied fifteen standards to this criterion and posed certain questions. Let us now begin to develop answers.

Standard 1. The HRD Function Has the Ability to Diagnose Problems and Anticipate Needs

What are methods for gaining the close relationship that will allow access to organizational data? To be effective, the HRD function must have access to organizational data. The function must be able to identify the needs of its customer (the larger organization) in order to meet them, and this cannot be done without access to the larger organization. Here are some methods for gaining the relationship that will allow for this access:

1. Involve members of the larger organization in various types of active HRD planning and advisory committees and boards. Use the people who can help you, and use the people who might potentially place barriers in your way. If you are planning a needs analysis, identify a committee of subject matter experts and put them together with HRD staff to identify target areas, then use your experts to set up field contacts or even collect and review data. The old adage "People support what they help create" is never more true than the HRD advisory board of field managers in a large organization!

2. See that information on HRD function capabilities and successful programs and projects gets to the larger organization on a regular basis. If you want access to organizational data, you sometimes have to model the process first. Have HRD open houses; invite specific managers and put on formal presentations and demonstrations. Put out newsletters on your activities; let people know who is in the organization so that when you call a district manager to interview a number of her people for a task analysis, she knows your HRD function and what it is you do.

3. Volunteer for task forces and committees that will put you and your people into close working relationships with managers from other functions.

4. Call managers you need to know and invite them to lunch or set up an appointment to go see them to talk about the HRD function and its role in the larger organization.

How can trust be achieved to allow the HRD function into the larger organization to collect necessary data? This is another of those chicken and egg situations; once an HRD function has demonstrated its value to the larger organization, it will usually be trusted again. In the early stages of HRD function development, trust is achieved best on a one-to-one basis: personnel who make up the HRD function are perceived as trustworthy, either because they have demonstrated competence in some way (advanced degrees, articles or books published, field experience) or even more specifically, because one significant manager in the larger organization knows and trusts an HRD employee on a personal basis.

Trust is also built up program by program. Each successful activity is a step up the ladder. Trust is an elusive commodity, built partially on fact and partially on perception. It can be enhanced or destroyed over time. Effective HRD organizations are aware of the need to maintain organizational trust and sensitive to activities that can destroy it.

Standard 2. The HRD Function Is Supported by a Corporate HRD Mission Statement or Organizational Culture

How can the HRD function ensure that its mission statement and an understanding of its purpose are clearly understood at all levels and across all subunits of the organization? First, draft an HRD mission statement, using a process that involves the total HRD organization and makes sure that the HRD mission statement is in line with the larger organization's mission and goals. Once this is done, the HRD function can use a variety of means to achieve understanding:

1. Publish the HRD mission statement in internal publications and request feedback.
2. Send the mission statement to key line and staff managers for feedback.
3. Take the time to meet with people from the larger organization who do not seem to understand the HRD function, to clarify and explain just what you are about and how you can support them.

Standard 3. The HRD Function Has a Commitment to a Strategic Planning and Supporting Organizational Change

How can the HRD staff first get involved in strategic planning?

1. Ask to be involved; ask up the line until you reach the decision makers. Make the request in the form of *why* this will benefit the larger organization. Requests for involvement in planning efforts appear to be self-serving unless they are supported by data that is as strong as you can possibly make it. Cite facts and figures. You may be able to identify specific problems—and costs—that the HRD function was called on to "fix" which might have been avoided had you been involved in strategic planning.

2. Develop your own strategic plan, and communicate it throughout the larger organization.

What can the HRD staff do to stay involved? If you understand the purpose and process of strategic planning, make a contribution to the process, and understand the politics in your specific organization regarding strategic planning, you will continue to be involved. If you overlook any one of these factors, you will decrease your value to the organization and also your chances of staying involved in the process.

Standard 4. The Roles and Responsibilities of the HRD Staff Are Clearly Defined

How can the HRD staff best model the role and responsibility definition process for the larger organization?

1. By defining roles and responsibilities within the HRD function, documenting the process used, developing models, and communicating this model process to the larger organization through identified communications channels.

2. By actually training units of the larger organization in the use of the model process, if this is a need of the larger organization.

Standard 5. The HRD Function Has Commitment to Front-End Analysis and Evaluation

How can line and staff management be involved in front-end analysis? How can they be involved in ongoing evaluations?

Line and staff management are the keystone to accurate data collection. Unless (as we discuss in Chapter Six) there is a real understanding by line and staff management of the need to support front-end analysis, the HRD function will not be allowed into the larger organization to collect the data necessary to support the larger organization.

By now, you realize that an underlying theme of our research findings and of this book is the need to involve line and staff management in every *appropriate* step of everything the HRD function does. To be involved in front-end analysis activities, they must first understand what these activities are and how they will affect the outcomes of the HRD function. Here is where the HRD function's ability to meet its customer's needs is totally dependent on the customer's clear understanding of the full HRD process—and front-end analysis in particular.

One organization with which we are familiar is a good example. People in the field understand the need for the HRD function to get into the field to conduct needs and task analyses to target scarce training dollars on the most critical needs, but the larger organization is in a fight to the death over market share for its products, and sales managers find it really difficult to spare even an hour or two of valuable staff time to talk to HRD personnel. So the HRD personnel go out into the field and ride with the sales representatives for a day, a week, or whatever its takes to get the information needed. It is then fed back to line management for validation before going to staff management for final signoff.

Involving line and staff management in data collection in the field, and asking them to spend time away from the crush of their day-to-day work requires a fine balance and a sensitivity on the part of the HRD function to the reality of field pressures. We have found it is easier to ask people to evaluate HRD activities after they have been completed, than to ask for time "up front" for the type of analyses necessary to really meet the needs of the larger organization. Both are possible, however, if the HRD function takes the time to understand the organization it serves.

Standard 6. The HRD Function Has Strong Commitment to Staff Development

What role does management play in HRD staff development? In effective HRD functions, staff development is built in to the annual operating plan as a requirement. It is not only supported by management, but seen as essential to the continued effective operation of the HRD function, and it is supported by adequate funding.

Is staff development integrated into performance evaluations, and if so, how? In a number of HRD functions, staff development is now an identified performance objective for all personnel. When an objective-based performance system is used, where staff write their own performance objectives and then negotiate these with their management, specific staff development activities are spelled out based on personnel development needs and anticipated organizational requirements. When this process is integrated with operational planning, budgets are established for the developmental activities.

Although most HRD functions that use this process renegotiate performance objectives at three- or six-month intervals, bringing them into line with the reality of the organization as it changes, staff development objectives are generally adhered to unless a sudden and unanticipated need emerges that can be met in no way other than to change staff development targets.

Standard 7. The HRD Function Is Perceived as an Internal Consultant to Management

What kinds of legitimate "networking" activities can the HRD staff perform with line and staff management to institutionalize the function as viable internal consultants?

1. Open up the doors of the HRD function in formal open houses and demonstrations of function capabilities.
2. Listen; make competent HRD function personnel available to listen to the problems and needs of line and staff.

3. Problem solve with line and staff; meet the HRD function's customer needs, even if it means going outside the HRD function or even the company to do so; act as a broker if necessary to meet customer needs.

Standard 8. The HRD Function Has a Strong Marketing and Public Relations Capability

Should the HRD function market to line and staff management? If marketing is what is required to make the HRD function effective, then yes, absolutely! Some of our study respondents said that they did market on a systematic basis, and some said that they did no marketing whatsoever. We suspect that those who say they do no overt marketing to line and staff management probably use other means to publicize their capabilities and expertise, or perhaps the culture of their organizations enables the type of communications that makes overt marketing superfluous. The fact is, if the HRD function is not known, used, and respected, it is not effective.

Standard 9. Members of the HRD Staff Are Perceived as Experts

What role does the relationship between the HRD function and line and staff management play in the larger organization's perception of the HRD function as experts? There are apparently two key elements in the development and maintenance of the "expert" perception of the HRD function by the larger organization. One, as we mentioned earlier, has a direct connection to the relationship between the HRD function and line and staff— it is based on one-on-one relationships between HRD staff and other managers. If a line or staff manager knows personally and perceives an HRD person as expert in his or her field, this contributes to the overall perception.

The second element has to do with what the HRD function produces rather than any type of relationship. If the products successfully meet the needs of the larger organization, the function is perceived as expert, or at least as having experts within it. If the function does not meet the needs of the larger organization, no matter how expert the people within it supposedly are, they will eventually not be perceived as such.

Standard 10. There Is a High Level of HRD Staff Teamwork, Creativity, and Flexibility

Can teamwork, creativity, and flexibility occur in HRD functions when these elements are not present in the larger organization? Yes, of course they can. It is more difficult to build a unit that is flexible and creative within a rigid organization that does not reward (and may even punish) creativity, but it is possible—and necessary. In his work on applied creative thinking, Ned Herrmann teaches the principle of "making your own space" within a larger organization. Effective HRD functions frequently exist within organizations that, by virtue of their size alone, are more structured. The HRD function *must* retain its creativity and flexibility to efficiently meet customer needs. As far as teamwork is concerned, this is an essential element of *any* HRD function; its existence should not be affected by the lack of it in the larger organization.

How can close HRD function relationships with line and staff management help line and staff to be more creative and flexible? By discussing modeling behavior, and demonstrating evidence of benefit for the modeled behavior. By developing the level of trust in the modeled behavior through one-on-one relationships.

Standard 11. There Is a High Level of Ethical Conduct Among HRD Staff

Where should HRD staff loyalties lie—to the profession or the organization? Both! We see no need to compromise. If HRD staff is asked by the larger organization to undertake an effort that is not professionally sound, it is probably not in the best interests of the larger organization either. The difficult part of this issue is pointing this out in a tactful way.

*Standard 12. The HRD Function Is Perceived as
"Part of the Business"*

*What is the balance in effective HRD functions between
being perceived by line and staff as professional and being perceived by staff as "field relevant" or "part of the business"?* This is
not an easy question to answer, and appears to differ from organization to organization. In many HRD functions today, staff
have emerged from the line and, having found themselves in (or
even managing) an HRD function, have gone back to colleges
and universities to gain the professional knowledge needed to
perform effectively in the function.

At the same time, more and more "professionals" are now
in the workplace: instructional designers and writers with master's degrees, HRD managers with advanced degrees in adult education, human resource development, or management science.

The bottom line is apparently that effective HRD functions *are* perceived as "part of the business" because they either
get their people into the field regularly, use subject matter
experts from the field, or both. They are also perceived as
"professional" because they seek out and hire key people with
advanced degrees in HRD and adult learning. Both are necessary.

*Standard 13. There Is a High Level of Congruence Between
HRD Function Goals and Objectives and Goals and
Objectives of the Larger Organization*

*Is the congruence a direct result of the close relationship of
line and staff management to the HRD function?* To a certain
degree, it is. But it is also caused by the HRD function's understanding that such congruence is necessary in order for it to
support the larger organization effectively and efficiently.

*Standard 14. The Function Is Perceived as Conducting
Reality-Based Programs*

*What is the relationship between the function being per-
ceived as conducting reality-based programs and the degree of*

HRD functional relationship with line and staff management? We believe that there is a direct relationship. It comes partially from the one-on-one relationship between function personnel and line and staff personnel. Word-of-mouth communications between friends (HRD and field) often initiate some type of front-end analysis that frequently uncovers real needs that the HRD function can meet.

We have noted, too, that when there is a stong relationship between HRD function personnel and the field, HRD personnel tend to spend more time in the field, and this in itself generates further identification and refinement of real field needs.

Standard 15. There Is a High Level of Networking with All Levels of Management

How can a new HRD function develop these "network relationships"? Almost everything we have talked about in this chapter can be initiated by a new function to some degree: setting up task forces and advisory committees; identifying with top management goals and objectives, and letting management know you are doing this; volunteering to support all sorts of activities, from corporate strategic planning (which, we realize, may *not* be an invitational process) to working with the company's Little League team. Market, get the word out on your new function, ask for input on your plans and processes, eat in the staff dining room with different people every day. There is no one way, and no right way; there is only the necessity to develop these relationships in order to be truly effective.

6

A Highly Professional HRD Staff

Perhaps the most valuable result of all education is
the ability to make yourself do the thing you have to
do, when it ought to be done, whether you like it or
not; it is the first lesson that ought to be learned;
and however early a man's training begins, it is probably the last lesson that he learns thoroughly. . . . The
great end of life is not knowledge but action.
———Thomas Henry Huxley,
"On University
Education," 1876, and
"Technical Education,"
1877

We were not surprised that the second criterion that emerged
from our research was the need for a highly professional staff.
We did not, however, anticipate as much tension as we found
in discussions of professionalism. "Professionals" in human
resource development in the late 1980s must prepare themselves
differently for a wider range of roles and responsibilities than
they had five to ten years ago, and the dichotomy that frequently
occurs between the "professionally correct" decision and the
bottom-line decision can sometimes be difficult for HRD professionals to deal with.

In 1979, Leonard Nadler wrote:

The person responsible for human resource development is probably the single most crucial factor
affecting the role, but there is still lacking sufficient understanding of who or what this person is.
Various attempts have been made to identify him

and to draw a composite picture. No one picture emerges, but what does become apparent is that the persons responsible for HRD usually come to the position with a variety of backgrounds and skills, with little of the background having been planned in anticipation of an HRD assignment.

The engineer, the personnel director, the controller—all have some commonality of academic backgrounds which prepare them for the position. The human resource developer is more like the executive who comes to this high post from a variety of backgrounds. The difference is that the executive is not expected to perform in a specialized area but as a generalist. The HR developer may need some of the abilities of the generalist but requires something more to accomplish his functions as a specialist. . . . It is unlikely that the HR developer has had an organized program leading toward this position . . . there is no agreement on the academic experience which would be appropriate [p. 161].

This last statement may, in part, still be true today: there is little agreement on the appropriate academic experience, although most human resource professionals in the 1980s have had the benefit of some organized program. We found, however, that "professionalism" in HRD includes a number of dimensions that were not considered just five years ago. These now include a heavy emphasis on the traditional business skills, for instance. In addition, "professionalism" in human resource development today includes not only advanced degrees in HRD (and all the knowledge the particular educational program may impart), but also experience in the field. It also includes:

1. Understanding of the industry you serve.
2. Understanding of current technological change, its potential impact on your industry.
3. Ability to address strategic business needs.

4. Ability to solve problems creatively, coupled with a high level of diagnostic skills.
5. Leadership skills.
6. A reality-based orientation, combined with a sense of the future.

The "highly professional HRD staff" described by our respondents embodies a combination of expertise and power—expertise in the form of knowledge to efficiently, effectively, and creatively meet organizational needs, and the power to implement solutions.

It sounds deceptively simple. It is not simple: leading, not dragging; strengthening, not discouraging; opening the way and not conducting to the end—and doing it all when it ought to be done whether you like it or not—all that takes consummate skill as well as courage in this complex world in which we ply our trade. We can no longer be "specialists" in human resource development alone; it just is not enough. The key HRD people in any organization today must understand the totality of the business they are in.

Elements of Professionalism

In this chapter, we look at this complex issue of HRD professionalism: what it means today to people who are operating professionally in effective functions, and what these people feel is necessary in order to *be* professional.

Knowing Your Business. Robert Desatnick (1984) cites four factors as the differences between successful and credible human resources functions and those that fall short.

1. Understanding the business.
2. Addressing strategic business needs.
3. Positioning the function as a top management discipline.
4. Measuring and improving their own effectiveness.

Note that "understanding the business" tops the list. Our study respondents agreed with Desatnick that the human resource professional *must* understand the business because the human resource function cuts across and serves the total business. Desatnick wrote:

> The importance of understanding the business is underscored in a survey of 125 senior line executives conducted jointly by the American Society for Personnel Administration and Towers, Perrin, Foster and Crosby. The study cited a broader perspective and greater knowledge of the business as one of the most important training and development needs for human resource professionals. . . . In the 26 companies reviewed there were examples of both successes and failures of the human resource function. Both occurred regardless of the size of the company, the nature of the industry and whether or not a union was present. The survey included companies that were growing, declining and remaining stable.
>
> An example is the human resource professional at General Electric. Human resource trainees experience three years of intensive training in a variety of functions. Typically, they are given six assignments over a three-year period, including full-time project work in engineering, finance, marketing and manufacturing, plus being assigned to other non-personnel functions.
>
> The review showed that other successful human resource executives acquired this broad knowledge and understanding of the business in a variety of ways. . . . In each situation, the senior human resource executive first spent a great deal of time learning the business. Most studied the financial reports, the strategic business and marketing plans and the objectives of each major function. They met at length with senior officers, noting priorities of those functions and the human resource function [p. 42].

At Xerox, the HRD professional with both advanced degrees *and* line experience has some advantage over the HRD person with only professional credentials. "When I was in the branch (or district)" is used as a badge of honor. In fact, line experience alone often has more credibility in a human resource function than professional credentials alone. We present this as a fact, and not a goal. As a matter of practice, these types of people (with no HRD experience) tend to treat all their responsibilities equally, either neglecting professionalism for day-to-day nitty-gritty activities or neglecting really important business needs. They are so busy that they suffer from too many, often conflicting priorities. They seldom allocate sufficient time to address needs seriously. Desatnick talks about how necessary it is for successful human resource executives to think, speak, and act like senior line managers. By inculcating a bottom-line orientation, they avoid attempting to be all things to all people; they do not overcommit or raise false expectations. They divest themselves of activities that others can do as well or better and seem to have a fetish for honoring their commitments. They promise only what they can deliver and they deliver what they promise with the highest standards of professional excellence and timeliness.

Kenneth Ewing of Hershey Chocolate told us, "I have been with the company for over fifteen years. I used to be the manager of staffing and development but I have also worked in several other areas." Ewing believes his knowledge of his company is a significant contributor to his function's ability to deliver effective training programs.

Rosabeth Moss Kanter talked about the role of human resource professionals in what she terms "integrative action"— the willingness to move beyond received wisdom, to combine ideas from unconnected courses, to embrace change as an opportunity to test limits (Galagan, 1984). She discussed how the leading-edge human resource departments are working as partners with line management in guiding change and see themselves as serving the needs of the organization rather than simply developing the perfect training program. They are much more field-oriented; in several companies it is the human resource people who mastermind those kinds of projects and who act as the key facilitators and resources. They are helping make sure that top management, whether divisional or corporate, functions as a team. They encourage bringing in every perspective and thinking about the whole problem. That puts the key human resource person in the position of having to understand the whole business and going beyond his or her specialty.

Training and Development Journal published a discussion (Bové, 1985) of whether HRD directors should have a training background; the participants seemed to answer the question with a "yes, but. . . ." Samuel H. Phifer, executive training director for Allied Stores Corporation, noted that it is important that HRD directors have an understanding of the concepts and methodology of training, but questioned whether that should be their only qualification. He points out that if you are in a large organization, you need managerial ability. You need to know how to run an organization, and that means running your own training organization and probably even some line experience; you need to know the technology of your industry. Good training people should have an authoritative, noncoercive managerial style. They have to be pacesetters to do their own thing, and be democratic in style. A good training director should have the kind of profile a good executive has.

Our respondents said that the manager of an effective HRD function knows what the business is really all about, as well as the philosophies and policies of the company's top people. And, they said, if their fundamental managerial philosophy offends you, do not try to sway or convert them. If you are having trouble changing lower level executives' attitudes, value systems, and behaviors, imagine the impossibility of doing anything like this at the top. If you are really offended on valid ethical grounds, don't sulk—get out.

Thomas J. Newman, corporate director of training for Johnson's Wax, said, "My background gives me bias, but I think HRD directors should start out as trainers. A director of training needs some business experience—either rotational experience in the company or an outside MBA . . . that gives the person more credibility than, say, a person with a master's degree in training. One of the best trainers I have ever met got his undergraduate degree in education and his master's in accounting. . . . There is an overall need for the director of training to understand the corporate philosophy and approach and acceptance of training within the company."

Maria C. Clay, director of training and organization development at the North Carolina Memorial Hospital in Chapel Hill, talked about knowing your organization. "None of [our] training department members had a health care background, so the first two years were spent getting to know the organization: how the hospital is organized; how it is financed; what its products are; who works there and what they do. . . . After two years of educating ourselves, the health care professionals came to respect the training people and the work we do with them. But you cannot provide service if you do not know your organization thoroughly."

Peggy Hutcheson, Atlanta Resource Consultants, says that HRD professionals who are really serious need to look at themselves as business people who happen to be in the human resource and development profession. Hutcheson believes that focus is critical for practitioners if they are to be credible in their organizations, "linked in with the mainstream of the organization."

Finally, on this subject, Thomas Gutteridge, dean of the college of business administration and professor of management at Southern Illinois University at Carbondale, wrote this in response to the question, What steps can HRD practitioners take to develop themselves professionally? "Focus on getting breadth as opposed to simple depth. HRD people need to develop beyond their particular skills and competencies. They need to do so clearly within the HRD field, but not to the exclusion of developing some breadth—breadth in terms of understanding the function outside the HRD area. For example, spend a period within another function or get assigned to a task force that takes you into, say, the marketing or production area. But you really need to have a good understanding of how the organization is structured and what the roles of other functions are."

Generally, our respondents said that you need to pick up a pretty good bottom-line orientation in terms of understanding finance, return on investment, and marketing. This is the business end that the line people you interact with already have.

The HRD professional today must see the broader perspective. There is within most organizations a much broader human resource management function that must be addressed. It involves not only human resource development and career development, but also human resource planning and forecasting and other activities concerned with recruiting, allocating, motivating, and compensating the organization's people resources. The professional HRD practitioner must understand how all these activities work together.

Both study respondents and current literature agree that, to be effective, human resource professionals today must know their own business as well as current business practice. But there is more to opening the way than simply unlatching the gate through knowledge of your business.

Developing Good Management Skills. Almost as serious a problem as the line manager who becomes manager of a human resource department as a "reward" with no knowledge of the human resource profession, is the trainer who finds herself setting up or managing a human resource function with little or no management training or experience. Our respondents repeatedly told us that the ability to manage effectively is a significant contributor to the effectiveness of an HRD function. To them, this means understanding the basic management skills of planning, organizing, leading, and controlling, and also the underlying skills of listening, communicating, and delegating.

Effective human resource functions apparently tend to work with a team framework whenever possible, maintain a high level of trust and openness, and share their information openly as a matter of policy. Effective human resource managers are frequently risk takers, but in a calculated and knowledgeable sense—they do not put their function on the line capriciously, nor do they operate in a vacuum apart from their staffs. They spend a lot of time seeking information and listening to their people, in essence, being guided in a very real way by the expertise they have working for them. Their people feel valued by this behavior, and the win-win of this participative management contributes to the function's effectiveness.

There appears to be an atmosphere of fun in many of these effective organizations; managers don't take themselves too seriously, and consequently their staffs feel supported and not "managed." They all share in the goals and objectives of their function, and understand their place in the support of their organization.

Understanding Technology Changes. Many of our survey respondents talked about being both proactive and pragmatic. In this era of frantic technological change, the challenge for human resource practitioners can be overwhelming. To analyze and understand the impact of technological change on your own industry, much less the larger society in which we live, means studying not only the physical environments in which we live and work but also changing values.

We all know that the office of today does not look like the office of even five years ago, and communication, information management, manufacturing, and even sales systems are changing almost monthly. Knowing *how* to use such things as computers, electronic communications, teleconferencing, video discs and compact disc technology to manage your business and to train is as critically important today as knowing *when* to use this technology.

Hutcheson and Stump (1984) predicted accurately:

> The simplicity of the technological issues is evident when we look at profits. Technology will create new jobs: people will have to make it, service it and train others how to use it. At the same time, machines will take over jobs that won't be replaced. The expectation that tasks will get done more quickly, less expensively and with fewer errors is almost always the organization's motive for investment in technology. It is too early to tell exactly what the balance will be between job losses and gains.

What we do know about the technology explosion is that it continues to change basic parts of our lives. Changes are taking place in the way we learn. Classrooms with instructors are being supplemented by computers and interactive video disks. Holographic instruction may not be far away.

Changes are taking place in the ways we earn our livings. Entire new industries are emerging. And existing businesses do business differently. Today's buzzwords are entrepreneurship and "intrapreneurship."

Changes are being made in the way we manage. Ready accessibility of information means new roles for managers and a reduction in the layers of management. In many businesses, middle managers are left out of streamlined organization structures [p. 68].

At Xerox, we are aware that technological change is the main force now driving education and training. In order to remain competitive in our highly competitive marketplace, we no longer train the "nice to know." Our courses are increasingly "needs driven," based on attempts to improve performance rather than employee satisfaction.

A recent study by Towers, Perry, Foster, and Crosby (American Society for Training and Development, 1986) shows that managing the business in times of change is a chief concern reflected in the types of training and development offered. Productivity improvement, motivation in a slow growth economy, managing and training technical talent, and motivating when career options and rewards are limited are all training growth areas.

This same report cites major factors affecting corporations today—technology, the shift to an information-based economy, and international competition—that are influencing the content of training and development programs, which more often than in the past supported specific company goals. "Where technological superiority is a goal, training efforts focus on the skills and knowledge of technical personnel. Technical skills updating, along with information-age skills, are cited frequently as important growth areas. 'More and more of our jobs call for knowledge-workers,' says an energy company trainer. Typists are learning to use word processors; sales clerks to operate computerized cash registers; plant workers to use computer-controlled equipment. Communication training is increasing, particularly when it is tied to the development and transmission of corporate culture and to better motivation through performance appraisal" (p. 15).

Perhaps one of the greatest frustrations and fears of the human resource professional who has been a practitioner for more than five years is (and will probably continue to be for the foreseeable future) the need to know about new training technologies, to be out there on the cutting edge. Computer-based training is increasing, although more slowly than many expected five years ago. As the costs of travel combine with removing people from the work site for days and weeks, more and more companies are looking at ways to use distributed training technologies in the most appropriate manner. "Training delivered with the help of some form of technology is often easier to control, sometimes cheaper to deliver, more easily kept up-to-date, and is more responsive to individual needs. As its benefits appreciate, its use will grow" (p. 15).

Artificial intelligence technology and "knowledge-based systems" are being viewed as a way of learning more about how adults learn. But how is the human resource practitioner, too frequently bogged down in day-to-day survival activities, able to reach out and grow? Our organizational survey produced many comments such as "I know I need to develop my technological skills [or knowledge], but right now I just don't have the time!"

There are no easy answers, although Hutcheson and Stump provide some valuable and, in our experience, viable recommendations:

> We must continue growing. We must ensure that we and those around us have time and energy to grow. We cannot help others grow if we are not pursuing growth ourselves.

We must work together. The tasks before us are too big for any one person or professional group to tackle. Our networks will become more and more active, channeling energies from disparate sources to nudge the institutions we serve.

We must know how to make sense of chaos. As the forces of change advance, there will be moments—sometimes extended—of chaos. We must be able to take this confusion and move forward.

We must take the lead in meeting our future, yet remain conscious that life is likely to play tricks on us. Things will not happen as planned. Recognize these as opportunities to move forward with our visions [pp. 70-71].

Maintaining a Realistic Results Orientation. One of our study respondents put this aspect of human resource professionalism in an effective organization succinctly: "Don't train more than you need to; know who you are and who you aren't."

The Xerox Leadership Through Quality program, which is significantly changing the culture of the corporation, is based on a worldwide mission statement that features "meeting customer needs." This means first finding out what customer requirements are (a basic prerequisite to meeting customer needs, but one we sometimes forget in human resource development functions) and then meeting them accurately: giving customers exactly what they need, not less and not more.

Dana Robinson, president of Partners in Change, Pittsburgh, concurred (Bové, 1986). She thinks that you really have to begin looking toward a results orientation more than an activity orientation. You need to be able to report to management on what you are doing in terms of how the organization gets back $7.50 from every dollar it spends. She feels it is a rare program that can report those kinds of results—the sort of behavior and knowledge growth as a result of these developmental efforts that management can see as organizational benefits.

Another respondent noted that being realistic (results oriented) means understanding your organization as it is, its constraints, culture, history, and climate. If production requirements mean that managers have only half a day for a workshop, take the half day and provide the maximum amount of training you can cover reasonably in that time. Accommodating your organization's constraints (which always exist) and introducing your line and staff personnel to ideas they can truly use will earn an HRD function an image of being responsive to what managers want and need.

Being idealistic is important for advancing the field, but when you need to get a program up and running to make money, you need to be realistic. Nine times out of ten, training that meets the organization's needs will satisfy yours too.

Many of our survey respondents told us that the HRD professional *must* be reality- and results-driven, that it is absolutely necessary today for the effective human resource practitioner to think, speak, and act like line management. Desatnick describes this behavior as avoiding technocratic language and developing your staff to do likewise. By inculcating a bottom-line orientation, you avoid attempting to be all things to all people. You do not attempt to do the line manager's job. Instead you provide management with tools and methods to improve effectiveness.

But let us go back to the dilemma we presented at the beginning of this chapter: Given the need for a business and results-driven orientation, how does the effective and professional practitioner today balance bottom-line business needs with professionalism when a business-based decision may not, in his professional judgment, be in the best interests of learners? What happens when learner needs and business needs collide?

We believe (and our survey respondents supported this belief) that pragmatism is the bridge between professional and bottom-line differences in the real world. If you are not there, you cannot provide anything for the organization. However, if your value system is violated to the extent that you are rendered ineffective, then get out. Hanging out in an organization where you are ineffective can be the most unprofessional behavior of all. "Easy for you to say"—is that your response? Both authors have experienced the frustrations one endures when personal value system and organizational value system are out of sync, and we have both left positions that rendered us ineffective in this way or did not fulfill us professionally. These decisions are not easy, and you are the only one who can make them for you; but if we are talking about professionalism in the real world, there must be a balance between business needs and professional values within which you, the HRD practitioner, can function.

Maintaining Creativity: Keeping Your Sense of Humor. This aspect of professionalism was mentioned by our respondents frequently enough to warrant attention. Maintaining creativity appears to be somewhat difficult in larger organizations, where standardization of processes is frequently seen as much more desirable than expressions of creativity, which are often perceived as more "costly." This perception may have to do with the culture of the organization or with the organization's experiences with what has been labeled "creativity," but a number of our survey respondents talked about the need to remain creative, have fun, and take risks.

As Charlie Fields ("Profile: Charles Fields," 1986, p. 6) says, "You have to be willing to take risks. If you are too wrapped up in loyalty and security you can become almost useless to your company. You don't have to be a wide-eyed radical or revolutionary to bring about change; you can take it with common sense, but you can't be paralyzed by fear of rocking the boat."

Ned Herrmann, formerly of General Electric Corporation and the acknowledged guru of applied brain research in the human resource development field, talks about the necessity for building your own creative space in an organization. Herrmann believes that creativity is essential to effective behavior in and outside the workplace, and his research, his workshops, and his life support this belief. One of our respondents told us, "If I can't be creative and have some fun in my work, I can't be effective—it's as simple as that!" It may not always be so easy to achieve, but many effective human resource professionals believe that creativity and its attributes are essential.

Highly Professional Staff—The Model

Let us now turn to the questions we posed in the HRD Effectiveness Model relating to the second criterion: a highly professional HRD staff.

Standard 1. The HRD Function Has the Ability to Diagnose Problems and Anticipate Needs

What kind of expertise is needed? For example, the ability to diagnose organizational and individual problems and recommend appropriate solutions. Yes, diagnostic ability is critical. This means the ability to use a much more sophisticated system of front-end and needs analysis than most human resource practitioners currently practice. Front-end analysis has become a technical tool over the past ten years, evolving from work originated by the military and incorporating job/task analysis and computer-generated systems.

Diagnostic ability also involves understanding the wide variety of human resource issues and needs that change with the condition of your business, possibly the state of the economy, and certainly the level of skill and knowledge of your organization's personnel. The professionally competent human resource staff will be able to select the most critical business needs in their organizations, establish appropriate priorities, and identify appropriate solutions. This comes back again to knowing your business as well as the most appropriate diagnostic tools—which can mean, for instance, using mail surveys, line personnel in advisory committees, or telephone interviews when the state of the business will not allow enough travel to provide on-site data collection.

It also means that the professional staff do understand the need to establish correct priorities and do not "shotgun" their efforts or treat all their responsibilities equally. Critical business problems must be their first concern. Solutions must be based on the needs of the organization *at the time.* An organization we are familiar with spent a lot of time and money attempting to implement a quality-circle process at a time when it was also going through a reduction in force. The quality-circle process failed dismally because people were afraid for their own jobs and simply did not care about expending effort on problem solving when they might not be around to reap the benefits. If you understand your business, then the data you collect in a diagnostic process will point to potential solutions.

How is needed competence achieved? By all the activities you are familiar with: graduate programs in human resource development provide the baseline information; reading current publications and attending professional conferences keep you up to date; networking with other professionals through personal and professional meetings, seminars, and so on help you test your knowledge against others' experience; and getting out there and doing the work tells you what works for you. There is no easy way, and no single source of information, but rather a myriad of opportunities. We might add one word of caution too: it is very easy to become isolated and insulated within an organization. "Groupthink" is real. Without the continual seeking, searching, and testing of new concepts and ideas outside your own organization, you can start to believe your own press releases! Professional human resource practitioners maintain and nurture professional as well as business knowledge through contacts outside their function and organization.

Standard 2. The HRD Function Is Supported by a Corporate HRD Mission Statement or Organizational Culture

How can the HRD professional staff facilitate the development of an HRD mission statement? Easy: if none exists, write one. If no corporate mission statement exists, volunteer to write that too, and incorporate the HRD statement into it. If a corporate mission statement does exist and it does not reflect in any way the human resource development aspect of your business, study it to determine if an amendment is possible in the context of your business, and if it is, recommend it. But above all, lead by modeling behavior: create and live by an HRD mission statement. If you do not know why your function exists, how can you expect the organization to accept you? If your organization does not understand and value your function, you cannot be effective.

Can the HRD staff influence organizational culture? Of course. By understanding the current culture, identifying and prioritizing the changes that are needed to improve business practice and increase productivity, and making thoughtful recommendations to senior management, the HRD staff can be a most powerful influence on the culture of the organization. By modeling identified new behaviors, the HRD staff can also influence organizational culture in powerful ways. By implementing processes and conducting programs directed to needed culture change, the HRD staff can be the single most effective means of organizational culture change.

Standard 3. The HRD Function Has a Commitment to Strategic Planning and Supporting Organizational Change

How can professional staff be better prepared to support strategic planning and organizational change? In our research and our experience, we have found that few human resource development programs, inside or outside institutions of higher education, provide knowledge or skill practice in strategic planning. Traditionally strategic planning courses are provided by schools of business and business administration. As educators, we have come to strategic planning rather late in the game, but knowledge of strategic planning processes and their elements is as critical to today's effective human resource development staff as knowledge of the business, diagnostic skills, creativity, and an understanding of adult learning.

Courses and seminars are being offered by some large consulting firms and many colleges and universities today, and we urge the human resource practitioner who has not had this type of training to seek it. Consider it an investment in your future and the future of your organization. As one of our respondents said, "You have to know what senior management is talking about when it comes to strategic planning if you want to stay in the ball game!"

Standard 4. The Roles and Responsibilities of HRD Staff Are Clearly Defined

What techniques and resources are available to facilitate this process? Using your knowledge of your business and starting with your human resource function mission statement, identify operational objectives—what must your function produce in terms of outputs over the next twelve months to fulfill the mission statement in the context of the strategic business objectives of your organization?

You can use the American Society for Training and Development's "Models for Excellence" publication to identify the roles and responsibilities required to meet each objective for your function. This does not necessarily mean that you have these people on staff. Carry out this exercise without specific people in mind. You should have:

1. Strategic business objectives for your organization.
2. Mission statement for your HRD function.
3. Operational objectives for your HRD function.
4. Roles and responsibilities identified in order to carry out the operational objectives that support the strategic business objectives of your organization.

Now you can review your staff competencies against the workforce needs you have identified, pinpoint gaps, and either schedule professional development activities for current staff, identify new head count needed, or negotiate with management to limit the strategic business objectives. This should take place each year as part of your organization's strategic planning process. Until you define your function's manpower needs in terms of the competencies needed to support your business, you will always be subject to the whims of senior management and their view of your function, and you cannot be fully effective unless you are very clear about the competencies you need to support your organization.

Standard 5. The HRD Function Has a Commitment to
Front-End Analysis and Evaluation

What specific competencies and skills are required in today's organizations to conduct front-end analyses and evaluation? We mentioned under Standard 1 the need to understand both the theory and technology of front-end analysis, job/task analysis, and training needs analysis. Many human resource professionals today are confused about the difference between job/task analysis and training needs analysis; they are not the same, and the terms should not be used interchangeably. Job/ task analysis is a sophisticated process of breaking jobs down to a task level that is finite enough to attach standards for performance and collect data on the frequency, difficulty, and importance of each task. Effective human resource professionals know when to use this technology, and how to apply it most effectively in their organization.

Training needs analysis is the process of data collection within an organization to determine training needs, and this can be done in a variety of ways using a variety of tools. Evaluation of training in effective organizations can be based on the specific behavioral objectives of identified training needs, on pre/post testing, on observation of on-the-job training. It can be formative (process evaluation) or summative (product evaluation). It is *always* conducted for the purpose of making decisions about a human resource intervention: to continue the intervention, to change it, or discontinue it. Both front-end analysis and evaluation are theory-based, have a variety of tools available, and are carried out for the sole purpose of improving the accuracy, efficiency, and effectiveness of the products of the human resource function.

How can the HRD function develop these skills and competencies in staff? Once needed competencies have been identified, higher education courses, seminars, workshops, and professional publications are available. The trick for the HRD manager attempting to build staff competencies is to focus and truly identify the objectives of a given learning opportunity. Do not just send staff to workshops based on a workshop title or even its stated objectives. Ask the professor or seminar leader for past participants you can call to find out exactly what the workshop or seminar or course did teach. In this era of tight training dollars, make very sure you and your staff are going to get exactly what they need from your valuable dollars and time.

Are valid instructional design principles and processes used and understood by all personnel? We believe that this question must be answered totally in the affirmative for a human resource function to be effective. You may be running or working in a small function (you may be a one-person function, for that matter) that contracts all of your training, but you still must understand instructional design in order to purchase valid programs. If you are working in or managing a function that actually designs instruction, this is an absolute need. We have found human resource functions managed by line managers who do not understand instructional design, and they are seldom, if ever, effective until the line managers become knowledgeable about the business (the HR function) they are running.

As human resource professionals become more competent managers as well as professional practitioners, we will see less and less of the one- to two-year line manager assignment to run the HR function. Until that time, it is imperative that personnel involved in the human resource function understand instructional design; you don't necessarily have to do it, but you do have to understand the principles.

Standard 6. The Function Has a Strong Commitment to HRD Staff Development

Do effective HRD functions "make" or "buy" professionalism? Both. Professionalism is "made" by creating opportunities for staff development and by building professional competence within existing staff; professionalism is "bought" by bringing in competent consultants or packaged programs. Both are appropriate strategies, depending on the situation and available resources.

How is staff development managed for maximum efficiency and effectiveness? Effective human resource functions are fairly pragmatic these days; staff development activities are generally tied directly to the business needs of the organization and the competency needs of the function, and less and less to general developmental or motivational needs of individual employees.

How are personal and organizational goals aligned in effective HRD organizations? In many effective organizations the alignment of goals is achieved by:

1. Identification and clear definition of organizational goals by HRD management.
2. Identification and definition of personal goals by all HRD personnel.
3. Negotiation between HRD staff and management of alignment through objective-setting.

People in effective functions frequently are given information about organizational goals when they are interviewing for jobs, and are able to discuss with HRD management whether or not there is a fit. In cases where people have been moved into functions without this information, annual goal and objective setting provide the forum for discussion. As we keep emphasizing, this alignment is necessary *to some degree* if individuals are to be even minimally effective. If you find yourself in an organization that has goals you cannot in good faith accept, you cannot be effective. Sometimes the trick is in recognizing that this dysfunction is happening to you.

An HRD consultant we know was working for a research and development firm that was awarded a significant military contract having to do with weapons development. Our friend's value system required that he could no longer work for the firm under these circumstances, and on completion of his immediate project, he resigned. This is a clear-cut example. It is more difficult when you find yourself doing work that you really never intended to do: writing curriculum materials for products that do not seem useful, when you really want to be designing training aimed at helping people function more effectively in a new high-tech environment. You may need to recognize that your organization does not care how people function, and if you cannot help to create the culture that supports the work you feel needs to be done, then it may be time to seek other employment.

Standard 7. The HRD Function Is Perceived as an Internal Consultant to Management

What types of professional development activities prepare HRD staff to function as internal consultants to management? There are a wide variety of courses in institutions of higher education today, a significant number of seminars on consulting, and even some that focus on the HRD professional as an internal consultant. A good way to start this professional development process would be, once again, to identify the objectives of your function, then determine what internal consulting skills are required to fulfill the objectives. Once this is done, you will have a specific checklist of needed skill and knowledge with which to "shop" for developmental activities.

It may be that the literature (books and journal articles) will meet your needs. Perhaps one or more professional meetings or conference sessions will provide all you need; you may want to seek information from peers who are working in this type of situation. Or you really may need a seminar or college course. It will depend on your own evaluation of your current skill and knowledge against the requirements of your current or planned position.

How can the internal consulting capability best be communicated to management? If you have matched your capabilities to management needs, then proposing projects based on the requirements of your customer (management) should be your next step. Selling your capabilities to management is always easier when you have a track record to run on, and we talk about track record building in the next chapter. The operative word is *perception.*

The perception of value can be communicated overtly through memos, publications, demonstrations, and volunteered support activities. The communication can also be achieved through informal channels, the types of networking activities we discussed earlier. There is no "best" way to communicate your capability; anything that can get the information out into your organization is fair.

Standard 8. The HRD Function Has a Strong Marketing and Public Relations Capability

Are there ethical limits to marketing professional staff? There are ethical limits to marketing anything if the project does not live up to its advertisements. While marketing and public relations are a matter of survival for most human resource functions, you have to be very clear about what you are marketing. Do not promise what you cannot deliver. Scope projects with as much accuracy as possible; attempt to meet your customer requirements accurately. Understand your market as well as the skills and capabilities of your professional staff; make sure you can deliver what you advertise—on time and within budget.

How can marketing and public relations capabilities be developed? Build your knowledge base through courses, workshops, and readings, then get in touch with a local public relations firm or the public relations function of your organization and ask to pay a "field visit" to conduct an informational interview. Structure a list of questions you need to formulate a marketing plan for your function, such as:

1. What media have you found most useful to reach people in this organization, locality, or environment?
2. Given the kinds of work we are capable of doing and the goals of our organization, how would you recommend presenting our function?

Ask your friends in marketing how they would present your function and its capabilities to senior management, then develop a marketing plan and ask them to critique it. You should know best how to communicate within your organizational culture, but the marketing people can help you put the selling edge on your ideas. Do not be afraid to ask for feedback on your ideas in this area; external HRD consultants are out there selling all the time—tap into their expertise.

Standard 9. Members of the HRD Staff Are Perceived as Experts

Can this be done without a highly professional staff? We really have to waffle a bit on this question. Real-world experience tells us that it can be done, for limited periods of time, if your staff is articulate in the business of the organization or if you are lucky enough to contract out for consultants or programs that happen to meet your organization's strategic business needs (there are more "articulate incompetents" in significant positions in American industry than we will ever know). Maintaining the perception of professional expertise over time when it is actually absent is another question. Eventually the lack of competence will catch up with the HRD function, and when that happens, any perception of expertise quickly disappears along with credibility.

The only guarantee for maintaining an effective HRD function over time, a function that truly serves the organization of which it is a part, is the continued development of professional staff competence. In many effective organizations, this means developing competence in specialized areas such as instructional design for computer-based training, task analysis or sophisticated evaluation; in other effective organizations, it means developing more general management and management training skills; in still others it means research and development. Whatever the needs of the organization, the effective human resource development function must provide professionally competent staff to ensure that they are met, and because needs are always a moving target, changing and evolving, professional development of HRD staff must be an ongoing process.

Standard 10. There Is a High Level of HRD Staff Teamwork, Creativity, and Flexibility

Are creativity, teamwork, and flexibility a result of professionalism? We believe they are very much a result of professionalism in our field. There are certainly people who are instinctively creative, and there are people who instinctively create team-oriented and flexible environments in which to work; but the ability to maintain your own creative space, to build and maintain functioning teams who work flexibly in highly structured organizations, takes skill, knowledge, and experience. It is not easy to even maintain your sense of humor when a tight economy presses in upon your organization and the organizational stress descends on your function.

Professional HRD practitioners take time to study human behavior; they know the theory and dynamics of organizational behavior as well, and in their ongoing personal development efforts continually seek new ways to lead and motivate.

Do effective HRD functions spend time developing teamwork, creativity, and flexibility? Absolutely! Although the majority of time is spent on helping people learn to work as team players, managers of effective HRD functions do seem to create a work environment that supports and rewards creativity—which means that their people are allowed to take risks and be creative without fear of punishment for failure.

Several years ago one of us was asked to conduct a performance analysis of a major division of the corporation we worked for, and one of our primary findings was (not surprisingly) that the company expected *quality* work of all employees, but rewarded employees only for *quantity.* In that environment, creativity and flexibility were actually punished, because such behavior was perceived as not adhering to company standards— and if you didn't adhere to standards, you could not produce the *quantity* required in everyone's annual operating plan. We were called in to conduct the performance analysis because all sorts of processes were not working and productivity was devastated. Unfortunately, with rewards only for producing quantity, and real punishment for the kinds of creative behaviors that would produce quality as well, the bottom line was in a state of major erosion. We were able to introduce the concept of rewards for creativity and creative problem solving, and the culture of that organization is slowly changing, but the lesson was a difficult one.

Effective human resource development functions *model* behavior for their organizations. Perhaps the most important areas an HRD function can model for its organization are those of teamworking, creativity, and flexibility.

Standard 11. There Is a High Level of Ethical Conduct Among HRD Staff

Is there a relationship between professionalism and ethical conduct; is either necessary to the other? Yes, there is a relationship between professionalism and ethical conduct. Although it is certainly possible to conduct yourself ethically without being a professional HRD practitioner, we do not believe that it is possible to be a *professional* HRD practitioner and at the same time behave unethically. Professionalism may not be necessary to ethical conduct, but ethical conduct is absolutely essential to professionalism.

Ethical conduct in effective human resource functions is demonstrated by such simple things as giving credit where it is due, such as management recognition of all staff who have contributed to a successful effort, or just accurate citations in company publications. We are always surprised to find in-house training packages incorporating work—without appropriate credit—we recognize as having been done outside that organization. Ethical conduct also means accurate costing of HRD function-developed products, paying consultants in a timely manner, and delivering promised products on time and within budget.

Standard 12. The HRD Function Is Perceived as "Part of the Business"

What types of professional development activities for HRD staff are required to ensure that the function is perceived as

"part of the business"? Tom Gutteridge's recommendations
(cited earlier) are a good framework for these types of developmental activities. He talked about getting breadth as opposed to
simply depth, spending time in other functions of your organization, or getting assigned to a task force or special project that
takes you into another area such as marketing, finance, or
production.

We recently talked to a colleague, Chip Bell, who said he
had spent the previous day "riding around" with a client. In
Xerox, people in HRD functions attempt to spend as much
time as possible in the field, riding with sales or technical
representatives to better understand their jobs or to conduct
task analyses. We have spent weeks at a time following systems
analysts around, helping them install machines and throw
cable, asking why they do what they do. We have spent months
at a time in the field, analyzing the work of customer administration—order entry, machine and contract control, and billing
functions—to make recommendations for revised work systems
or training.

The staff of effective HRD functions spend time understanding clearly the strategic business plans of their organization, how the personnel compensation and finance functions
work, and how their own function fits into the whole of the
organization. They understand business, and they understand
their business; they do not propose projects that are not clearly
aligned with their organization's goals and strategic objectives.

Standard 13. There Is a High Level of Congruence Between the HRD Function and Organizational Goals and Objectives

*In effective HRD functions, is the congruence a direct result
of HRD professional development?* We believe that it is. If we
take a look at what it takes to make the congruence a reality in
an organization, it is difficult to believe that it could happen
very often by chance. To develop this congruence between the
HRD function goals and objectives and organizational goals
and objectives, it is necessary to:

1. Identify and clarify organizational goals and objectives—which can mean, as we have pointed out, that you may have to help your organization actually develop a goal or mission statement. In order for the HRD function to work toward supporting this organizational mission statement, it is also useful to have some type of actual outcome embedded in it.
2. Based on the organization's mission statement, identify and clarify the requirements for an HRD function mission statement, including outcomes.
3. Identify the roles and competencies needed by the HRD staff to carry out the functional mission statement and achieve the outcomes. And the staff had better be professionally developed to ensure that the outcomes are achieved. You can look really congruent on paper, but if you cannot deliver, you are going to be in trouble.

Standard 14. The Function Is Perceived as Conducting
Reality-Based Programs

Is this dependent on an HRD professional staff, or can reality-based programs be bought "off the shelf"? Certainly reality-based programs can be bought "off the shelf"; there are many companies today specializing in fine programs that can be bought and used as is, or tailored to meet your organization's needs. The trick is knowing clearly what your organization's specific needs are, then being able to assess and evaluate off-the-shelf programs accurately to be very sure that they will produce the desired results.

The needs analysis and program evaluation activities required do involve professional skills, although it is possible that as a new HRD function, you may also want to purchase these activities as well. At some point, however, professionally trained HRD personnel—whether outside or inside your organization—must conduct the required activities. How you go about acquiring these professional skills will depend on your knowledge and experience, the level of professional knowledge and experience of your staff, your budget, and your organization's HRD requirements.

Standard 15. There Is a High Level of Networking with All Levels of Management

Do professional practitioners network more easily with other professionals than with management? Not necessarily, but HRD practitioners who have studied and practiced in the field to the point that they can really consider themselves "professional" have been in graduate programs and seminars where many networks start. They have taken part in professional association activities where they have connected with other professionals, and they have built their support networks within the HRD profession.

At the same time, this experience of building and maintaining support networks does provide HRD practitioners with a model for working with all levels of management within their own organization. In effective HRD functions, the professional staff understands the need to build these networks—up, down, and across the organization. It is an interesting phenomenon, however, that HRD people network with other HRD people and line managers network with line managers, but line managers seldom seek out HRD people to include in their networks. The responsibility for setting up these networks frequently defaults to HRD personnel—which is fine, as long as we recognize that networking is important if we are to be effective, and that we have to do it.

7

Building a Track Record

Badness you can get easily, in quantity: the road is smooth, and it lies close by. But in front of excellence the immortal gods have put sweat, and long and steep is the way to it, and rough at first. But when you come to the top, then it is easy, even though it is hard.
—— Hesiod, *The Theogony*, circa 700 B.C.

The third criterion essential for an effective HRD organization that we identified through our research is the ability to build and maintain a track record of high-quality products and services. These activities are inextricably linked to the other two criteria: professional staff, and a close relationship with management.

The first and most basic question we had to address in looking at the whole issue of track record building and maintenance is, where do you start? How do you establish the credibility of a track record when you do not have a track record?

The essential ingredients for building a track record are easy enough to identify:

1. Professional staff—the right people in the right jobs (meaning that, as an HRD manager, you resist the temptation to put your best instructional designer into the classroom when a trainer is needed, just because the designer is available at that moment).
2. A clear understanding of your larger organization's goals (meaning that your understanding is such that you are able to articulate the goals to your peers and staff).

3. Accurate front-end analysis to determine specifically the appropriate products or services required.
4. Production of the product on time and within budget.
5. Letting people know about your success.
6. Adequate resources to get the job done.

Looks easy enough, right? If it is, then why don't we all do it automatically? How *do* we do it? Why is it difficult? Is it really a chicken and egg situation? How much risk is (or must be) involved in track record building?

Track-Record Building Blocks

As we look at what people are doing in the field, some patterns—and some answers—begin to emerge.

Rock Turning. Marty Lewin at Allstate Insurance told us, "We were asked to prepare a seminar for a service area that submits new business. In preparing for the seminar, we discovered four major problems in procedures preventing new business from being submitted properly. At our suggestion, these problems were corrected. We [also] conducted a needs analysis and found a lot of inconsistent rules and a lot of errors in the home office."

This is the stuff that track records are built on: the HRD function is asked to do a relatively simple training task, and in using professional practice (front-end or needs analysis), discovers many more problems that are causing the organization performance problems—which usually have impact on the bottom line. When one rock is turned over, a multitude of opportunities emerges.

Bottom-Line Connecting. This may be one of the most powerful track record building mechanisms: linking the outputs of the HRD function to the organization's bottom line; proving to management that HRD function actions are critical to such areas as sales support, management development, product launch, quality of work life, technical training, and supervisory support. In the changing world we live in, it is difficult to conceive of an organization that will not be increasingly dependent on HRD; how well the function is able to track and demonstrate its value to organizational survival and growth will be a major determination of HRD credibility.

At the Perpetual American Bank, Gail George told us that the HRD staff gets actively involved in training that is recognized by the organization as being directly related to its business. Gail says that resources within the HRD function are "loose" enough to allow for immediate response to organizational problems, so they do not have to wait until the next planning cycle.

At Xerox, Gaery Rummler's "praxis model" for performance analysis was used for a number of years to link training to organization performance, because one of the significant outputs of the model was the ability to identify impacts on cash flow and actual income that resulted from a training need. (The model also places the employee in his or her own performance system and takes into consideration such things as consequences for behavior and feedback to the performer.)

At GEISCO (General Electric Information Systems Company), Frank Hart, director of education services, says that they "will do backflips to provide desired results." Frank notes that they do whatever is needed to provide training before the commercial release date of a new product to the public. He states emphatically, "There is a strong effort to quantify what has been done in training." They look specifically at the productivity and products delivered to outside clients and ensure that these results are shared in the organization.

Public Relations. We said earlier that "rave reviews" cannot be discounted; a very important part of building and maintaining a track record is letting the larger organization know about your successes as Frank Hart does. Here, informal networks as well as formal demonstrations, newsletters, or releases come into play. It really is important to get the word out; do not assume that anyone knows that what is coming out of the HRD function really has an impact on the larger organization. Tell them!

Over and over we heard the importance of sharing information. One training manager told us that in bad times as well as good, he could not think of any information that was ever withheld, either about the business or the HRD function within it. Good news was shared, but so was the bad.

Securing and Using Top Management Support and Line Accountability. At Harrah's Hotel and Casino, Jerry Denton says that line accountability has been the essential element in her track record building since she first arrived on the job in 1984. Before 1984, there was no successful training program in the company, according to Jerry. They had been using a packaged five-day program for new employees written by persons unknown many years earlier, and the one-person training department did all this. That was it for training.

When Mr. Harrah died, Holiday Inn bought the company. The new owners basically left the management structure (including the personnel) in place. They introduced the quality-of-work-life concept, and a training needs assessment was developed as a result. Eighteen topics were identified by a group of interdepartmental supervisors and managers. Work then began to develop curriculum or materials to address the identified topics. Jerry went in on a special assignment to work on this effort.

Jerry says, "Line accountability is my thing." She has always felt that training is a line function, and that first-line supervisors should be responsible. Each month she sends out a monthly schedule on what training will be offered during that month. Managers inform her who should attend which courses, and records are kept of who attends, which courses are most requested, and so on. Every course is developed from a needs base. In addition to ongoing interaction with the line managers, face-to-face surveys are conducted every six months to identify and meet future needs. In the HRD function at Harrah's, building a track record has meant ownership of training by both line *and* staff.

At Hewlett-Packard, Rick Justice, marketing manager at the systems marketing center, says, "We work to get consensus.

We can't *tell* them what they need, we've got to work together so that they see the importance."

"Our program differs from a lot of training," notes Leslie Agnello, training manager for the business computer sales center at Hewlett-Packard. "You don't get everything at once—that's not the way adults learn. You learn when you need to know. That's why we want product training out in the centers. You can't see from Cupertino what a rep in Knoxville needs to know." Since Hewlett-Packard was ranked as the third most admired corporation in America in a recent *Fortune* survey, and was voted by the survey's respondents as number one in "ability to attract, develop, and *keep* talented people," the HRD organization's ability to move with the larger organization is noteworthy—and evident.

At Loew's Corporation, Alan Monmeyer, director of manpower planning and development, says, "We don't market internally. We respond to requests. That puts ownership where it really ought to be—with management." The diversity of industries that make up Loew's makes the work of the corporate training department equally diverse and challenging. "Each division thinks of us as working for them, and we have to be accepted by people in different industries," notes Monmeyer. "They think they are unique and we respect that. We start where the client is at. We go in, learn the language, the culture and the management style. At any one time," he adds, "we are likely to be working on more than a dozen projects" (Lee, 1985, p. 45).

Monmeyer goes on to recount some examples of recent activities:

> They originally came to us and said they wanted an employee training program, but our assessment was that they needed formal systems in place before any training was done. This particular project involved more than simply putting together an operations manual. There was little agreement among division and theater managers on what the best procedure should be—how to collect tickets, what to do if the film breaks, how to handle a fire, etc. So the first order of business was to interview a cross section of

people in the organization, from vice presidents to
ushers, to find out what procedures were being
used. The training department then refined and
rewrote the procedures so that the theaters would
have a uniform "right" way of doing things. Division managers have been trained to introduce the
manual to individual theater managers by assigning
them to use the manual in their theaters to solve a
particular problem. The idea is to make the manual
a living, working document [p. 45].

Sam Gallucci, training manager at Congoleum Corporation, says, "I'm a sales-marketing-type person, and I'm not afraid
to put my neck on the line. My philosophy is that you don't
train for the sake of training: you train for productivity. If the
training department doesn't contribute to productivity and performance, it shouldn't be there."

But Gallucci has not taken any chances: he involved
employees—from the president on down—in seminars and training sessions, gradually building cooperation, credibility—and
the training department's budget. "I couldn't have done it without the in-house talent," he says, referring to the willing help of
subject-matter experts. "Now it's a piece of cake."

To implement his program, he trained four district sales
managers as trainers and took them on the road to train the balance of the district managers. "They had more credibility with
their peers than I did," he says. "I'm corporate. But the idea of
training coming from peers went over well" (Lee, 1983, p. 51).

Ed Robbins of Gelco Corporation states, "Our philosophy
is to give managers and executives the tools to develop their
people and solve performance problems. We're too small to do
all the actual training [Robbins and Rick Beresford, corporate
training manager, are the "lean and mean" corporate training
department], so we're very conscious of the return we get on our
training dollars. We try not to deliver what is not wanted. We
try not to deliver what is wanted but not needed. And we measure the results of our training and get good results" ("Profile:
Ed Robbins," 1986, p. 6).

Meeting Customer Needs: The Reality-Driven Function.
What are all these people really saying? What does a track record
really mean? For one thing, we believe that it means meeting
customer needs. Rosabeth Moss Kanter (Galagan, 1984) has said
that the leading-edge human resource departments are working
as partners with line management in guiding change, and they
see themselves as serving the needs of the organization rather
than simply developing the perfect training program. They are
much more field-oriented. They are often the people who bring
in the resources, who help management broaden their horizons.
They often create and facilitate the kind of cross-disciplinary
task forces or project teams that bring in new ideas.

Ed Robbins of Gelco says, "We try not to train unless we
absolutely have to; about 60 percent of the people who come to
us for training solutions are not faced with training problems. A
lot of problems are related to systems, environment and ability."
He continues, "When we do train, we incorporate programs
into how people are expected to operate normally. We don't tell
them to take two hours away from their desks for planning if
they can't leave their phones for more than fifteen minutes. And
when we do say no to training, we don't always just say no. We
say, 'these are the other things you can do first.' Or else we make
clear what their realistic expectations should be if we do the
training they request."

According to Robbins, "The big thing is keeping in mind
who our customers are and knowing our mission, why we exist
in the company. Our job is to help people improve and solve
performance problems so the company can be more successful. . . . We have gotten to know the business our company is in.
We don't sit in the ivory tower. Before we do any training for a
division, we spend time with the operating people. We get edu-
cated before we do any education."

Customized training to meet customer or client needs was
cited by Mahaliah Levine of Dean Witter Reynolds (Lee, 1984a)
as having a high payoff. Levine's people offer special workshops
tailored to the needs of special departments; they go in and talk
to them about their needs and problems. Levine says, "These
department workshops are among the training department's

most popular offerings—and they earned special kudos from the director of operations!" She attributed the employees' ability to survive a particularly heavy market volume per day in 1984 because of training.

Russell Young of Lomas and Nettleton notes that initially his department was careful not to "bite off more than it could chew" ("Profile: Russell Young, 1986). They began by developing a catalog of courses and selecting a few long-standing training problems to resolve. The department has evolved into a team of internal consultants charged, at least partially, with acting as change agents in this fast-growing company. Support for his efforts has always been strong, Young says. Senior management has always been concerned with training issues "and as long as we produce, carry out our mission and do what we can do to help the organization with the bottom line, we'll continue to have the opportunity to tell our story."

Chip Bell put it another way when he talked about being reality-driven as a necessary "seasoning" for training excellence: "Excellent training is congruent with the culture of the organization, the norms of the work group and the values of the individual ('at room temperature' so to speak). This does not mean that such culture and values are not altered, if appropriate, through training. It is recognition that the first step to competence change is to start where the learner is. As my friend Tony Putnam is fond of saying, it is easier to turn a mule after he is moving" (1983, p. 45). There is an important point here for all HRD functions: our organizations are *always* moving. If they are moving forward, then the credibility of our work and the value of the products we provide depend on our ability to truly understand this movement, and to anticipate field and market-related problems we can help solve.

If our organizations are not moving forward, they are probably moving backward or off center (for there is no stasis in nature or in organizations), and our job then becomes one of helping management to identify the HRD issues that we can work on. In large organizations the HRD function will find this complex situation easier by identifying and understanding

(1) the goal or mission of the larger organization, (2) the HRD mission or goal, and (3) field-relevant problems.

Training Is Seen as a Business. Another aspect of a reality-driven HRD function that is essential to building a track record is that training itself must be seen as a business. Leslie Agnello of Hewlett-Packard refers to the field training staff as a team. "Our team is different, our attitude is different," she says. "We see training as a business and we make business decisions. . . . We think of ourselves as a profit center: we present our contribution to division management along with other groups. We are measured on the results we show—more training provided more effectively; skills learned more quickly. Since field training functions in many ways as a sort of internal consulting team, one of its primary activities is selling itself and its services to the divisions. It's our job to help the divisions understand our overall strategy, and that involves a lot of persuasive presentations. We have a series of presentations that explain to the divisions how they will benefit from working with our team. You do a lot of that in a decentralized company that is made up of autonomous units!" (Lee, 1984b, pp. 25, 27.)

Front-End Analysis. Effective HRD organizations that really are in touch with the reality of their business environments do some type of front-end analysis. Robert Brinkerhoff made the point that even though the training courses are requested often and the classes are always full, we must still "bother" with front-end analysis because our survival as HRD practitioners is at stake. He writes: "In the evolution of a species, unneeded appendages or plumage are selected out and disappear. The same fate may await the HRD profession if it does not identify, serve, and demonstrate its impact on important organizational needs. In short, we can't afford not to do what is needed or to do what is not needed" (1986, p. 64).

Brinkerhoff says that available needs-analysis definitions and concepts are inadequate to serve the HRD goals of remediating performance weaknesses and deficits, enhancing strengths, seeking out and serving opportunities for greater performance, anticipating and avoiding future problems, and creating new strengths. He maintains what our research frequently found in effective HRD organizations—that the HRD function concerns itself with what is *right* in an organization as well as what is wrong. Brinkerhoff goes on to say that while discrepancies between expected or mandated performance levels and existing levels should be fixed, to expend HRD resources *only* on discrepancy needs is to ensure maintenance of the status quo.

We found front-end analysis done in a wide variety of ways; Xerox uses Mager, Rummler, and a number of other methodologies for conducting needs analysis, task analysis, performance analysis, and discrepancy analysis. Other companies use different strategies depending on the environment, current needs, and immediacy of feedback. Effective HRD organizations produce quality products that in turn produce track records because they plan and put time and effort up front into systematically finding out what the needs are for their products and services.

Buying Credibility and Benchmarks. Track records can also be purchased, if done in the right way. Kenneth Ewing at Hershey Chocolate Company told us, "We work very hard to ensure that our program is a success. We buy things that are established, tried, and successful. We check things out with others to find out what kind of success they have had with something before we buy it. For example, if we need something on negotiating, we go to a listing of the *Fortune* 500 companies. I try to find one that is similar to our company and then I call the HRD person to find out if they have done anything in that area, what kind of success they have had, etc." He continues, "A lot of our people get mass marketing flyers for all kinds of training. I keep folders with information on the different kinds of feedback I have gotten on it. This has proved to be very useful."

We have found that many managers of responsive and effective HRD functions build and maintain quality track records by a form of *benchmarking*—finding out what similar organizations with similar needs and problems have done, how well things have worked, and setting their own targets a little higher

Building a Track Record
97

and further out in time. Track records do not have to be built from scratch or from the ground up; reinventing wheels is generally a lose-lose proposition.

The question is apparently no longer "make or buy?" but rather, how can we best meet our organization and personnel needs? It may be a combination; it may be "buy," "buy and adapt," or "build."

At Ralston Purina, Tom Mundi told us that he uses an "Excellence" program: "We are using this packaged video program with our top managers all over the world. We spend a lot of time getting closer to the customer and it is rewarding. It is great for team building. We do one unit per month. [Our people] have thirty days to implement the program, but something usually starts within twenty-four hours of the presentation. We spend a whole day on each unit and do a lot of brainstorming. We try to get everyone involved—sales, production, etc."

Tom also uses a "Survey of Management Practices" program. He says, "We are making excellent progress in this area. We buy the questionnaires and scoring service from the vendor. The questionnaires are completed by managers, their supervisors, peers and subordinates. This provides them with good feedback on how they are perceived. . . . They receive their individual profiles that have been computer-scored and we discuss them with each individual. We talk about different management aspects and the importance of each. We also meet as a group and discuss group profiles. From that point on, we get into team building, which is custom built on the scores."

Mundi continues, "We have greatly expanded the area of performance planning, reviewing, and appraising programs, and reward and recognition based on performance against goals, strategies and mission. For example, we have what we call a 'performance pyramid' and have developed a book to use as a guide. This is the *first* step in our plan. We did videos to present this concept across the country. We usually take one full day for this first step and, as we work with each group, we brainstorm to determine the type of business our people are in. The most important thing is satisfied customers. Values are different in different parts of the world," he notes.

"Another important point that should be made is that we have fun!" says Mundi. "We have a lot of collateral materials like wall posters, wallet-size mission statements, rallies, hats, etc. We did a lot of work ourselves, but we did hire some outside consultants. Basically, we got top management to buy off after we did a two-hour presentation in which we provided all the details. The bottom line was return on investment. We showed them how cost effective this would be and they bought it. It has been very well received all around the world."

Having Fun—HRD as a "Court Jester." Before you scoff at the idea that not taking yourself too seriously can be significant in track record building and maintenance, think of organizations where people *do* seem to enjoy themselves and have fun; don't their products seem as credible as those organizations whose products and services emerge from deep seriousness? Is the Macintosh computer any less credible than any other just because the Macintosh design team had a marvelous time producing it?

Charles Fields at Hartford Steam Boiler believes humor can alleviate stress or "kill you" if handled improperly. Indeed, Fields likens his role as an internal consultant to that of a Middle Ages court jester. "A court jester wasn't just a buffoon or an entertainer. A jester was able to bring up sensitive issues with a certain immunity. He could be irreverent." Fields, the jester, was able to suggest that every time a job becomes vacant at Hartford Steam Boiler it should be totally reevaluated, not automatically refilled. He says, "You have to be willing to take risks. If you are too wrapped up in loyalty and security you can become almost useless to your company. You don't have to be a wide-eyed radical or revolutionary to bring about change: you can take it with common sense, but you can't be paralyzed by fear of rocking the boat" ("Profiles: Charles Fields," 1986, p. 6).

Track Records—The Model

Rock turning, bottom-line connecting, public relations, securing and using top management support and line accountability, meeting customer needs, appropriate front-end analysis, buying credibility (when it is appropriate), benchmarking, and even having fun—these are the kinds of things people are doing in the field to build and maintain track records of high-quality products and services.

Now let's take a look at the HRD Effectiveness Model and see if we can answer the questions posed about the third criterion: building and maintaining a track record of high-quality products and services.

Standard 1. The HRD Function Has the Ability to Diagnose Problems and Anticipate Needs

How can the HRD function make recommendations and deliver appropriate solutions to diagnosed problems?

1. By diagnosing accurately; using appropriate front-end analysis techniques and methodologies.
2. By using all formal and informal communication media available within the larger organization.
3. By buying or making the professional expertise necessary to identify the solutions and present them.

What is at stake when the needs are diagnosed correctly, but are not what the organization wants to hear? A lot—possibly the credibility of the HRD function if it does not report *tactfully* an accurate diagnosis. But, as Charles Fields of Hartford Steam Boiler said, "You have to be willing to take risks." You also have to know your own organization and what the climate will allow. It is possible to feed the accurate diagnosis in "pellet" form. But if you fail to report accurately, if you only tell your larger organization what it wants to hear when that means inaccurate data, you will *never*, in the long run, be able to build or maintain a track record of quality.

Standard 2. The HRD Function Is Supported by a Corporate HRD Mission Statement or Organizational Culture

What needs to be done to ensure that the HRD function's output is congruent with the mission statement? First of all, you have to be able to get your hands on the corporate mission statement; you might even have to facilitate the development of one. Once a mission statement is identified, you will then need to translate it into outcomes that are meaningful to the HRD organization. If the mission statement says that your company or organization will "meet customer needs," then what does this say to you in terms of outcomes? What kinds of front-end analyses are required? What is the observable evidence that a customer need is met? Who will be doing this? Finally, is training required to enable this set of outcomes?

Are some public relations efforts better than others? Obviously, but only you can make this decision. Quiet networking with senior management may be an ideal way to communicate HRD function outcomes in one organization; an "HRD Fair" might be the best way in another. The key here is that while you can produce marvelous products and services, you cannot really build a track record unless the decision makers in your organization see the value in what you are doing.

Standard 3. The HRD Function Has a Commitment to Strategic Planning and Supporting Organizational Change

What can the HRD staff produce to demonstrate commitment to strategic planning and organizational change? Models and recommendations for strategic planning processes, recommendations for organizational change based on thorough and professional front-end analysis.

Standard 4. The Roles and Responsibilities of the HRD Staff Are Clearly Defined

What are some of the ways to demonstrate payoff of clear role and responsibility definition to the larger organization? Publish the HRD staff roles and responsibilities, and how they were arrived at (the model) throughout the larger organization, then follow through: make it easy for people from the larger organization to do business with you.

Standard 5. The HRD Function Has a Commitment to
Front-End Analysis and Evaluation

How can time spent in front-end analysis and evaluation
be depicted to the larger organization as producing a valid return
on time invested in the effort? This really is a chicken and egg
issue. The best way to demonstrate a return on time invested is
to do a professional job of front-end analysis and evaluation
and demonstrate the payoff, then publicize it. This can require
the discipline of needs and task analysis, and pre- and post-
testing. If you have accurately identified a critical training need
and conducted the task analysis that allows you to write
behavioral objectives for the need, then you can develop pre-
and post-tests that statistically demonstrate needed behavioral
change.

If people return to their jobs from one hour or one month
of training that has been developed using good front-end analysis techniques and their performance improves, you need to do
the follow-up evaluation with supervisors, peers, and the training participants that will document the impact of this improved
performance. Then tell the organization about the process and
the product!

Can the HRD function correlate a financial return on
investment to front-end analysis and evaluation? It is not easy
because of the many confounding variables in any training situation. Carefully documenting time and staff hours spent in
course development *with* and *without* front-end analysis and the
results of each in terms of changes in learner performance on
the job is the ideal way to develop such correlations. In real life,
we seldom have the luxury to work with any type of control
group. The answer is yes, it can be done, but whether it is
feasible in any given organization is really situation-specific.
The Rummler model of performance analysis mentioned earlier,
which helps you look at current performance against an "ideal"
model, identify training needs, and assess the impact of *not*
doing the needed training, may be one of the clearest methodologies for this type of correlation.

*Standard 6. The HRD Function Has a Strong Commitment
to Staff Development*

*How can the HRD function show a direct connection
between professional products developed by staff and ongoing professional development?* By publicizing the products as well as the
professionalism of staff. It has been our experience that organizations *want* their HRD staff to be as professional as possible. If
an HRD function is producing professional products (products
that meet the organization's needs and are professionally developed and implemented), then it can, and should, use every possible communications channel to let the larger organization
know that the HRD staff is responsible and staying on the cutting edge through ongoing professional development.

As practitioners, we frequently forget that our motivation
for continued professional development is part of what organizations buy when they buy our services. Sometimes organizations
forget too that "you get what you pay for." Professional products
that meet organizational needs require ongoing professional
development on the part of HRD staff, a fact we all need to be
reminded of with some frequency.

*Standard 7. The HRD Function Is Perceived as an
Internal Consultant to Management*

*How can the HRD function capitalize on its track record to
establish itself as an internal consultant?* The fast path to credibility for an emerging consultant is through the door that a
training and development track record will open. Build small
successes around the organization and then capitalize on those
successes by approaching the managers and offering consulting
assistance. It may take some time before management starts to
call you when they need consulting help, but—especially in this
case—"slow and steady wins the race."

*Standard 8. The HRD Function Has a Strong Marketing
and Public Relations Capability*

*Is a track record dependent on public relations? Can an
HRD function establish a track record without marketing and PR*

activities? If so, how can this be done? The issue of public relations has been a broken record in our research; it reappears again and again. We have found that "formal" PR is not absolutely necessary, but some type of communication to and from the larger organization is absolutely critical. Call it public relations, marketing, networking, or selling—you cannot establish a track record unless you let the larger organization—your customer— know that you are meeting its needs.

Standard 9. Members of the HRD Staff Are Perceived as Experts

Can a track record be established if the HRD function is not perceived as a group of experts by the larger organization? Our research tells us that this is certainly possible. As long as the HRD function is made up of a group of professionally competent people who produce quality products that meet the larger organization's needs, they will eventually build this perception of expertise in their organization.

As you have no doubt realized by now, one critical ingredient of track record building is really knowing what you are doing. As our former professor, Dr. Leonard Nadler of George Washington University, says, "The difference between the professional and the nonprofessional is that the professional operates from a base of theory." If the HRD function is made up of a group of professionals who understand their field or discipline, their organization, and meet the needs of their customer (their organization), the perceptions of expertise will follow.

Standard 10. There Is a High Level of HRD Staff Teamwork, Creativity, and Flexibility

Do factors such as teamwork, creativity, and flexibility contribute to high-quality products and services in effective HRD organizations? An interesting trademark of effective HRD organizations seems to be their ability to produce quality products in all sorts of crisis situations because their personnel are able to think "outside the box" of their day-to-day organizational constraints and work effectively as teams. In the most effective organizations, roles are clearly defined, but it is acceptable to move out of them when required. Managers seem to manage through teamwork rather than authority, and people really do appear to enjoy their work.

We think this ability to work effectively as teams within an HRD function that rewards creativity rather than punishing it may be one of the most critical factors in the HRD function of the future. We are familiar with the HRD functions today that are managed by line managers who, because they are not professional HRD people, operate in a severely authoritarian mode, and these functions are not effective. As we move into an increasingly professional information-based culture where varied uses of new training technologies are the norm rather than the exception, the need for teamwork, creativity, and flexibility will have to increase if the HRD function is to become or remain effective.

Standard 11. There Is a High Level of Ethical Conduct. Among HRD Staff

Is it possible to produce high-quality products and services without a high level of ethical conduct? Both our research and common sense say an emphatic *no!* The types of unethical actions that might be considered (plagiarizing material is a good example) will, we are told, almost always catch up with the HRD function if not the person (who may have moved on by the time the plagiarism is discovered). The culture of an effective HRD function does not support or allow unethical conduct. It is simply unacceptable.

Standard 12. The HRD Function Is Perceived as "Part of the Business"

In effective HRD functions, how are quality products and services best produced as "part of the business"? This one calls for an "all of the above" answer. HRD products and services will be "part of the business" if:

1. Professional front-end analysis is undertaken and line and staff are involved in the front-end analyses and planning processes.

2. Measurement of HRD activities is established as a part of the front-end process and carried out.
3. The mission and charter of the larger organization are understood by the HRD function, and the activities are in alignment.
4. The measured results of the HRD function activities are communicated to the larger organization (and adequate feedback channels are provided).

If any of these items are eliminated, the guarantee of the HRD function being perceived as part of the business of the larger organization diminishes significantly.

Standard 13. There Is a High Level of Congruence Between HRD Function Goals and Objectives and the Goals and Objectives of the Larger Organization

What is the relationship between congruence and high-quality products and services? The relationship is not between congruence and quality HRD products and services, but rather between congruence and the *perception* of quality by the larger organization. The HRD function could be producing the highest "quality" products in terms of professional practice, but if they are not in alignment with the organization's goals and objectives, or if they simply do not meet the larger organization's needs, they will quickly be shot down as ineffective (and they *will* be ineffective).

We were frequently told of the frustrations experienced by HRD managers attempting to identify the mission or goals of the larger organizations they serve so that they can be sure that their own function's goals and objectives were in alignment. A number of people noted that helping their larger organization clearly define its mission and goals was a high priority for them.

The bottom line with regard to this issue is twofold: (1) the HRD function may need to facilitate mission/objectives definition for the larger organization to ensure that its own work is congruent with organizational mission; and (2) *only* if the

HRD function is meeting customer needs *and* its products and services are of high quality will the products and services be perceived as high quality.

Standard 14. The Function Is Perceived as Conducting Reality-Based Programs

Can a track record be established with anything other than reality-based programs? The respondents to our study do not seem to think so—and neither do we. If the HRD function is perceived as conducting reality-based programs, it will provide a solid foundation for building and establishing a reputation for quality.

Standard 15. There Is a High Level of Networking with All Levels of Management

How does "networking with all levels of management" con-tribute to the production of high-quality products and services? This is the informal communications link with the larger organization that can provide information on hidden agendas, roadblocks to production of quality products and services, and opportunities for new or unique services or products the HRD function might provide, not to mention the insight into the larger organization's politics and culture.

It is the ability of the HRD manager to call a friend at an appropriate level in management whenever she needs to know whether an issue surfaced by front-end analysis is "politically sensitive," and to test the waters on how best to handle the issue to create a win-win situation for the HRD function and the larger organization.

This type of networking usually comes with time and with involvement in non-HRD activities that involve cross-organizational teams or groups. Community service activities, staff dining-room discussions, noontime exercise classes, and employee involvement groups are all good mechanisms for net-working. So is walking down the hall and asking a colleague in another function to tell you about what he does.

No matter how it is done, our respondents and our experience clearly dictate the necessity to be able to tap into all available sources of information within the larger organization. The HRD function cannot work effectively within its larger organization unless all possible sources of communication are reasonably open. You may think you are doing fine, and suddenly a strategy comes booming in from left field that seriously affects a product you are three-quarters of the way through developing—when very frequently the informal networks knew about, and could have probably influenced, the strategy months before.

8

Developing a Plan
for Improvement:
Case Study

Awake . . . leave all meaner things
To low ambition and the pride of kings.
Let us, since life can little more supply
Than just to look about us, and to die,
Expatiate free o'er all this scene of man;
A mighty maze! but not without a plan.
———Alexander Pope,
Essay on Man, 1733–1734

It is a bad plan that admits no modification.
———Publilius Syrus,
Maxim 469, circa 42 B.C.

Let us assume you have taken the criteria and standards from the HRD Effectiveness Model and have evaluated your HRD function. Or maybe you are starting a brand-new function. You may even have just been hired to revitalize an organization's HRD function. How do you begin to implement the ideas that we have presented?

What you do *not* do is rush into trying to deal with the first problem you encounter or the first request a manager makes. What you do want to do is formulate a plan, a strategic action plan. This is a brief case study of how one HRD manager in a major division of a high-tech corporation developed such a plan. We hope this real example will help you through the HRD Effectiveness Improvement Process in the next chapter by demonstrating that it can be done.

Carolyn Weaver, manager of the HRD function for the systems division of Computer Sciences Corporation, was hired to take over an HRD activity that had been existing for years on a vague memory of past "good works" rather than present performance with the division. She found an HRD function that neglected off-site (field) offices' needs, conducted no real needs analysis, did not involve management, conducted contractual courses that were not on target, and did not deliver the training it promised. She formulated a strategy to change the credibility of the function and developed specific actions that would lead to her strategic goal. Her strategy consisted of two key elements:

1. A plan for the future based on her vision of an HRD function that was tightly linked to the organization's objectives and had line management commitment and involvement, an emphasis on practicality and high quality, and a professionally developed staff.
2. An immediate success story to ensure the support she would need for later activities.

Before she started planning, she spent a month walking around. She learned the organization's vocabulary, she listened to complaints about HRD, and she asked employees and managers what HRD might do to meet their needs. As Carolyn put it, "I listened to the system." She went to lunch with key managers. She asked questions about the organization culture. She tried to take a broad view—to see the whole picture rather than just look for training problems.

She discovered that performance appraisal was a "hot" problem. To scope out the problem, she did a complete literature search and also queried her professional network for alternative solutions. She designed and implemented a new performance review document in four months. And she worked with the compensation manager on the entire performance appraisal system and was able to satisfy just about all the complaints. In addition, a presentation was conducted for the president of the division and his senior staff, and training was delivered to all management as promised. She now had her immediate success story.

Carolyn found that one result of her success was that her department was perceived as a business partner with the line managers, yet that she was respected for her expertise as an HRD professional. She also decided to add two important items to her strategic action plan. The first was a way to give the system "deliverables"—tangible items like a report of the results of a special program or a monthly newsletter; these buy you time to do further planning. Too much planning and nothing tangible makes management suspicious; too little planning and too much emphasis on tangibles makes you look like a training factory.

The second new item was a decision to have all new HRD staff people take the same route that Carolyn did. Let them spend some time walking around, have them come up with a hot problem, and then have them "earn their spurs" while they were exploring how they fit into the HRD vision. Meanwhile, they would be collecting additional data about the organization that could help keep Carolyn's big picture up to date.

She and her staff added additional items to the action plan. All the staff would try to go to lunch with line people as much as possible (as well as still drop into offices to chat) to increase their organization network and keep it viable. They even located their offices next to an operational area, with Personnel on the other side. Line people would stop and talk as they walked through the area. They operationalized the idea of involving line management as trainers and found that the more management was involved, the more HRD was considered part of the business. Now Carolyn and her staff do not have to spend time convincing management that HRD is part of the system. In fact, it has become an honor for an employee or manager to be asked to do training.

The question of whether HRD should be part of Personnel is still controversial. Carolyn dealt with this issue by building a separate identity from Personnel rather than fighting to be structurally separate. They are part of Personnel and enjoy the benefits of that association but are physically separate (not in the same office suite) and have been able to establish an independent image. (We should note that Carolyn's human resource director does actively support HRD and shares Carolyn's vision and strategic orientation.) Working toward the vision and concentrating on actions that enable you to accomplish your strategy keep you from wasting energy on bureaucratic battles and fighting fires that are really not significant.

One "unwritten" part of Carolyn's strategy was twofold: (1) to encourage the organization to give employees more responsibility and (2) to help managers have more confidence in their abilities and their decisions.

Her needs analysis and her networking both pointed to three critical needs: leadership development, career development, and technical skills training. But Carolyn did not want to rush in with training because the organization had already been burned. She waited a year and a half to build the credibility of the HRD function while she developed an approach to meet all three needs. She developed an operating plan and identified a leadership development program to kick off the implementation of her plan.

First she set up a briefing for all of top management. (Before the meeting was conducted she discussed the program and her operating plan with the president of the division.) She asked the president to send a note to all the vice presidents. She then briefed the vice presidents and received their feedback. She lined up advocates from among the vice presidents and senior managers. She developed a briefing presentation. And then she held the meeting.

She put all her cards on the table; she started the briefing by talking about the HRD focus for the coming year. She laid out HRD's strategy, listed the activities planned to achieve that strategy, and explained how HRD was accountable for the results of those activities. HRD's goal of "performance change over time" was discussed. Carolyn described how HRD wanted to be perceived as an organizational resource, as responsive, as providers of an HRD *system,* not just events. She presented a systems model demonstrating that the training needed the active involvement of all levels in the organization throughout the program. She then discussed why leadership development was a key area and what outcomes this program would produce. The rest of the presentation concerned the program itself.

The planning that went into this presentation and the implementation of this program are especially noteworthy. Over and over again in our research we heard and read about the level of detail that effective HRD functions put into every aspect of their activities. Virtually nothing is taken for granted, slapped together, or rushed into just for the sake of expediency.

"It's the little things that count" is an apt saying for effective HRD. Lynn Moon, corporate training director for Duty-Free Shoppers (1986), uses actions such as these to solidify her department's position in her company:

1. Volunteer to do free pilot programs at outside locations. Select a location where you can expect a warm reception. Do a good job, then encourage that the word be spread.
2. Negotiate with vendors for free train-the-trainer sessions; their cost is small compared to the potential for business.
3. Volunteer to be a test location for vendors developing new materials.
4. Copy articles for managers. Coordinate group purchases for publications at reduced rates.
5. Create a resource library and publish a directory.

We could have filled a whole book with suggestions like these, because these are the kinds of actions effective HRD functions are doing while they are also running their programs, conducting other activities, and planning.

Carolyn Weaver found herself being asked to help a manager's son think about colleges and assisting a line employee write a résumé. These are the types of tasks many professionals would refuse to do (or are never even asked to do). They are not "dirty work"; they are a sign that she is an equal member of the informal organization. This kind of recognition is the kind that pays benefits when Carolyn needs help.

You have to start with a vision of what you want HRD to be in the organization. Then develop a strategy, formulate a plan to achieve that strategy, manage the actions of the plan, and evaluate the results. Only then are you on the road to HRD effectiveness.

9

The HRD Effectiveness
Improvement Process:
Putting the Whole
Picture Together

I love it when a plan comes together!
——Hannibal Smith,
"The A Team," 1985

The degree of effectiveness of the HRD function primarily
depends on the degree to which it becomes a responsive resource.
The level of responsiveness will be determined by the quality of
its staff (and management), its programs, and its organizational
relationships. The quality of these criteria will be driven by the
thoroughness of the planning and will be judged by the evaluation of its impact on the organization. In other words, what you
put into HRD is what you will get out of it.

You may have noticed the statement elsewhere in this
book that achieving HRD effectiveness is hard work. Effective
HRD functions are made, not born. Less than fully effective
functions *can* be improved. Figure 5 presents a process map that
depicts how to actually implement the standards and criteria of
the HRD Effectiveness Model. This flow chart literally walks
you through three phases of this process: planning, managing,
and evaluating effectiveness. In each phase you will see how the
elements of the process can and should be applied.

Figure 5. The HRD Effectiveness Improvement Process.

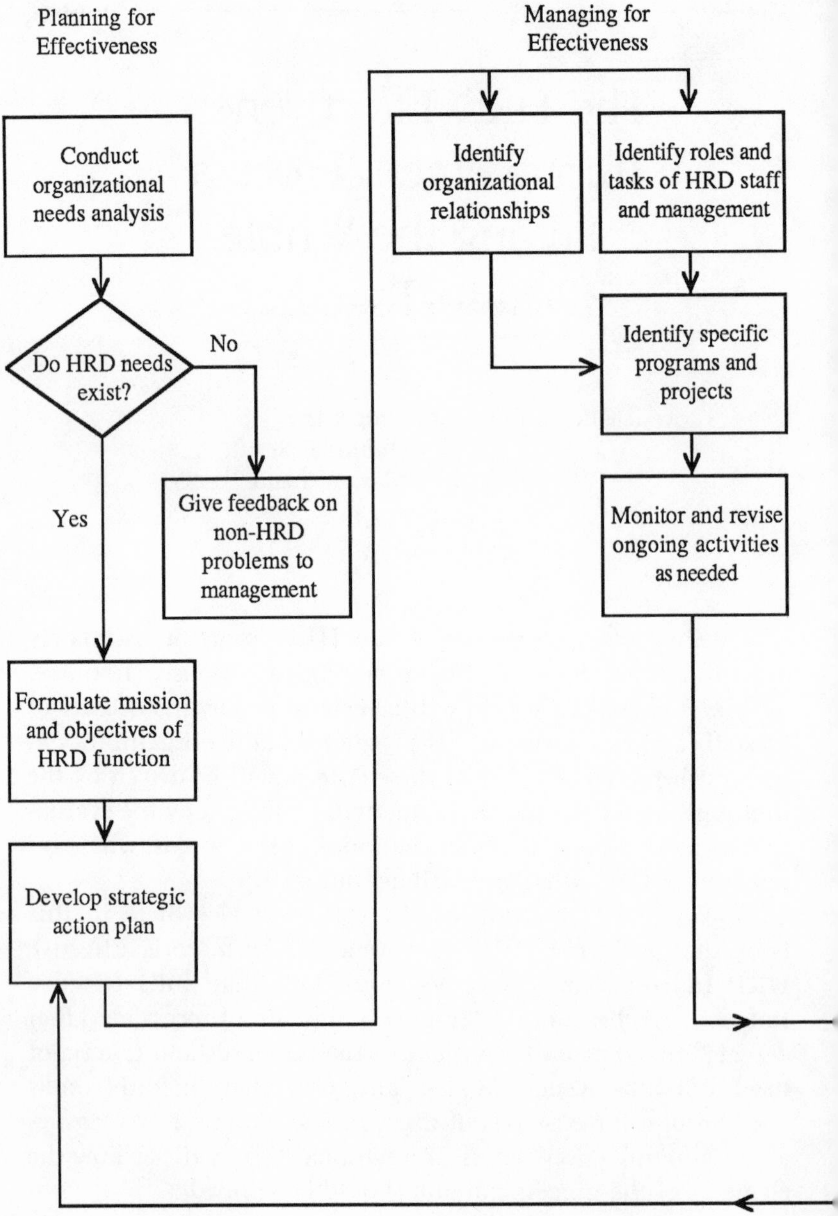

Planning for
Effectiveness

Managing for
Effectiveness

```
Conduct
organizational
needs analysis

Do HRD needs          No
exist?

Yes        Give feedback on
           non-HRD
           problems to
           management

Formulate mission
and objectives of
HRD function

Develop strategic
action plan

Identify
organizational
relationships

Identify roles and
tasks of HRD staff
and management

Identify specific
programs and
projects

Monitor and revise
ongoing activities
as needed
```

Figure 5. The HRD Effectiveness Improvement Process, Cont'd.

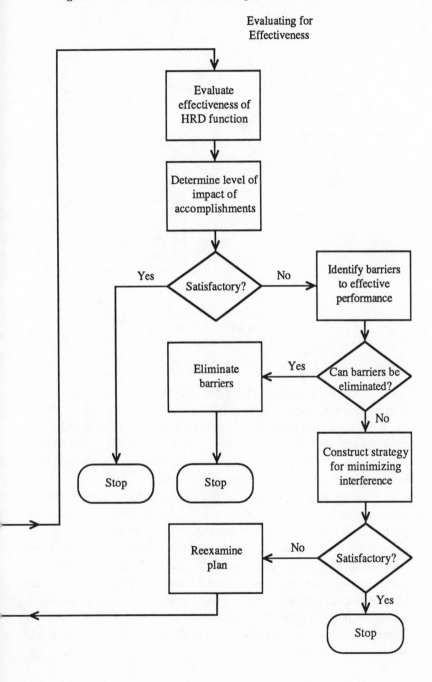

Planning for Effectiveness

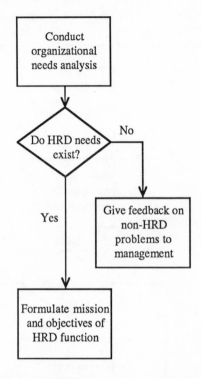

One of the critical elements of effectiveness clearly identified by our research is an organizational needs analysis to determine present and anticipated problems and opportunities. Once those needs are uncovered, you can use the HRD Effectiveness Model as a template to develop a mission statement for the HRD unit and identify its goals and objectives.

For example, a concern that the organization's word processing system is quickly approaching obsolescence would cause you to feed that information back to management. It *should* also cause you to think about whether you are perceived as an internal consultant by management (Standard 7) and whether you are perceived as experts (Standard 9), so that when the organization changes to a new, more sophisticated system you are called in to help the employees cope with the change. This in turn should link to the identification of Standards 7 and 9 as HRD functional objectives.

> Develop strategic
> action plan

The mission and objectives formulated for the HRD function should drive the development of the strategic action plan. The objective of becoming more of an internal consultant with expertise in sociotechnical approaches should translate into specific actions to achieve this objective. Your strategy may be to educate management about the sociotechnical approach and increase your visibility as internal consultants. The actions you plan may include conducting an executive briefing on sociotechnical systems, offering to assist a division of the organization that is changing over to a new hi-tech system, or developing a session on sociotechnical systems change and adding it to your management development program. (In this chapter we use the word *program* to mean either a major activity within HRD [such as the executive development program or the career development program] or the entire HRD function. *Program* in this case is much more than one course.)

Managing for Effectiveness

In order to carry out your strategic action plan successfully you need to take into account the three HRD effectiveness criteria:

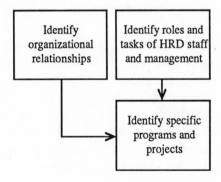

1. *Close relations with line and staff management.* Initiate a new network or improve on the existing one by setting up management-level steering committees and task forces. Ensure that the HRD function's priorities are based on top management's goals. Build an HRD network among specialists in other organizations in your industry or in your geographic area. Listen to people in your networks and their expertise.

2. *Highly professional HRD staff.* Ensure that your staff knows the business of the organization and can speak the language. Develop your staff so that they have as much expertise as possible; at the same time develop your own managerial skills to the optimum. Be constantly aware of changes in technology, both high technology in general and training technology in particular. Maintain a realistic, results orientation to your HRD activities. Finally, be as creative and risk-taking as possible.

3. *High-quality track record.* Conduct accurate and thorough front-end analysis. Link the outputs of the HRD function to the bottom line. Publicize your accomplishments. Build in both management support and accountability. Again, ensure that your programs are reality-based. Compare your activities with HRD functions in similar business and ask for their critiques of consultants and packaged programs. Lastly, have fun building your track record.

```
Monitor and revise
ongoing activities
as needed
```

Once you have built in the quality control, then you develop and conduct your programs and monitor them. Make midcourse corrections as needed. Let us continue our example of the need to build your expertise in sociotechnical systems and improve your visibility as internal consultants. During this phase your staff may do some reading on sociotechnical systems approaches to change or go to a workshop on consulting and change. You would also identify the key managers who are the most influential and can make or break your image as internal consultants. You would conduct the programs and sessions you developed on sociotechnical systems and do some short-term evaluations. Make sure to invite the key managers to these sessions and cultivate their involvement by asking them to review the sessions for you.

Evaluating for Effectiveness

Most HRD professionals believe in the evaluation of training and development activities; they may use reactionnaires on how well participants like a particular workshop, or a follow-up evaluation effort to measure behavioral change. However, evaluating courses is just one piece of the pie; it does not tell you if your HRD *function* is effective.

```
+------------------+
|     Evaluate     |
| effectiveness of |
|   HRD function   |
+------------------+
```

Steele (1973) cites two major purposes of program (function) evaluation:

1. To form judgments about programs using criteria or standards of comparison and descriptions of what occurred and resulted in the program.
2. To compare alternatives in reaching program decisions.

These two purposes may not at first seem to be different from course evaluation; the difference lies in the scope of the results. Evaluation that is concerned with overall effectiveness of a program deals with such elements as the balance in the types of employees reached, the extent to which the results deal with actual organization needs, and the efficiency of the organizational resources used. According to Steele, program evaluation is as concerned about the value and suitability of the program as it is with whether its purpose is accomplished.

There are two major approaches mentioned in the literature (scant as it is): descriptive and evaluative. Descriptive approaches, traditionally labeled *audits*, tend to describe what is; they review or examine the function and report findings. These findings may inform you of problems and inefficiencies in your function but do not necessarily help you identify the causes or the impact of the findings.

An extension of the traditional auditing procedure is the *performance audit*, which deals with problems, causes, and impact (Rothwell, 1984). A performance audit assesses how well results match intentions (effectiveness) and how well resource utilization matches results (efficiency). It answers such questions as:

1. Are the results consistent with the needs of the organization?
2. Are the results important?
3. Do they contribute more to the participants and the organization than if the resources had been invested in other things?
4. Were they produced at a reasonable cost?
5. Are the results sufficient in terms of the overall need?
6. If the results are insufficient, does it mean that the program is not effective or that changes need to be made in the way the program is carried out?
7. Are the results of one program significantly more valuable than those that could be produced through an alternative program with the same expenditure of resources (Steele, 1973)?

Performance auditing is a management tool that can provide HRD with the information needed to improve the effectiveness of the function (Bullock, 1981). It should be a normal part of the ongoing activities of the HRD function.

Performance audits compare present conditions to desirable criteria. While there are several examples of audit processes in the literature (Rothwell, 1984, and Tracey, 1974), there is very little mention of criteria. Rothwell's process uses an accounting-based audit model and his article mentions the need for criteria that are authoritative, credible, and convincing, but he never addresses how to develop the criteria. Tracey's process cites areas of concern rather than desirable criteria, although he does discuss the need for measuring accomplishments against objectives already developed for each program and activity.

This book is based on research that resulted in "desirable" criteria that can be used in a performance audit process. But we did not want to stop there, merely giving criteria and examples of how these criteria can be accomplished; we wanted to complete the picture by describing a performance audit process that can be used to evaluate and improve HRD effectiveness. The steps are based on a combination of performance analysis, auditing, and HRD management concepts and techniques.

```
+-------------------+
| Determine level of|
|     impact of     |
|  accomplishments  |
+-------------------+
```

This evaluation process is basically a form of discrepancy analysis (Provus, 1971). It is concerned with the impact of any discrepancy (positive or negative) between the criteria or standards and actual accomplishments.

The process assumes that:

- A program evaluation is warranted to make sound decisions on whether to improve, change, or maintain the HRD activities and practices.
- A problem-solving or goal-setting activity will be required to improve the HRD function.
- The HRD staff is committed to the change process required by the results of the evaluation.

Conducting the evaluation includes the following steps:

1. *Identify an evaluator or establish an evaluation team.* Ideally the evaluation should be conducted by someone outside the HRD function, preferably someone with program evaluation

or management auditing experience. Unfortunately, most of us cannot afford the luxury of an outside evaluator. The next best alternative is a small team composed of HRD professionals, with at least one person from another staff function and one person from a line unit. This mix of personnel will give the analysis added objectivity and give the results added credibility.

2. *Plan the evaluation effort activity.* Set up areas of responsibility for the team and time lines for the tasks. Ensure the availability of both needed documents and HRD staff. Share your plan with the HRD manager.

3. *Identify the HRD function's planned activities and outcomes.* These should be based on the goals and objectives of the HRD function, which in turn should have been based on the mission and goals of the organization. If the goals and objectives of the HRD function are not aligned with the mission and goals of the organization, then you already have one discrepancy that needs to be investigated.

The criteria and standards of the HRD Effectiveness Model should serve as a framework for establishing a new HRD unit's goals and objectives. They can also be used to derive individual objectives for an existing HRD function.

The HRD Effectiveness Model criteria and standards should stimulate the HRD unit's objectives or planned activities (whichever form you prefer). For instance, if after looking at the model, you decide that one priority you need to deal with is "close working relationships with line and staff management" and you decide that one activity you want to pursue is to establish a management steering committee, then this activity becomes the focus of the evaluation.

4. *Design an evaluation format.* Our suggestion is that you design your own format to actually conduct the evaluation.

5. *Conduct the evaluation and analyze the results.* Let's look at two scenarios of how this process would work.

- You're concerned about the level of professionalism of some of your HRD staff, so one of your planned activities is to send several of your staff to the upcoming HRD workshop on organization development (OD) skills. They go to the workshop and come back with a fairly sound theoretical approach to OD and some new ideas about combining OD and career development efforts. But they also come back with a concern that they really did not learn "skills"—more knowledge about techniques that with practice and experience will turn into skills. When the evaluation is conducted, the discrepancy between the outcome of learning new OD skills and the actual learning about techniques is noted. However, the staff now understands the theoretical basis for OD and is able to plan a new OD/career development effort, and that may be more significant in the long run in relation to raising the overall level of staff professionalism than the significance of not obtaining new OD "skills."

• You need a successful training program to begin to develop your credibility and realize that one of the immediate needs that surfaced out of the last needs analysis was a new program on customer relations. You plan the activity, involving line personnel in every step of the development process. The program is conducted and is very well received by the participants. You also include some follow-up transfer of learning efforts to ensure the success of the program. The evaluation is conducted. It is too early to tell if the program was successful in terms of improved customer relations, but the praise for involving line personnel in the program design has a very significant impact on your credibility.

The importance of any program evaluation is to get a holistic view of the effectiveness of the HRD function. You not only want to know if your activities and programs were successful, but also whether there were other ways the activities affected your effectiveness, whether there were unintended spinoffs from your activities, and what the implications are of all the findings. In determining the level of impact of your accomplishments, you look at both the specific changes and improvements and the long-term implications that resulted from the evaluation. HRD is a system, like any of the other organizational systems. You need to take a system's approach to identifying the interrelationship of all the short- and long-term findings.

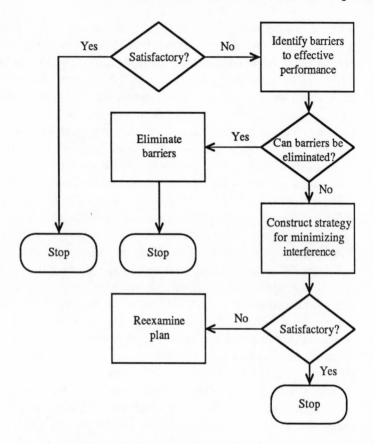

It is like throwing three pebbles in the water and watching how the ripples intersect. The idea is to step back and observe the intersecting ripples and get a total picture of the pattern they create. If everything is satisfactory, great! If not, can you identify the barriers and can they be eliminated or minimized? If you have done everything you can to try to improve the situation, then reexamine your strategic action plan to see if there were any problems you were not aware of at the time. Remember, we are not suggesting perfection, but thoroughness. To finish with our sociotechnical consulting example, this is when you want to step back and determine if you have been able to achieve the expertise and the image you wanted. The final proof would be whether you were called in to advise and work with the technical experts in designing and implementing a new word processing system.

The purpose of this HRD Effectiveness Improvement Process is to create, maintain, and improve your HRD function's credibility. Your actual achievements in helping the employees of your organization reach their highest potential, while you also help the organization itself adapt to change, is what HRD effectiveness is all about.

10

Anticipating Future Elements
of HRD Effectiveness

Lives of great men all remind us
We can make our lives sublime,
And, departing, leave behind us
Footprints on the sands of time.
—— Henry Wadsworth
Longfellow, *A Psalm of
Life,* 1893

Lend me the stone strength of the past
And I will lend you
The wings of the future, for I have them.
—— Robinson Jeffers,
*The Rock That Will
Be a Cornerstone,* 1924

We have identified a model of HRD effectiveness that we believe
will be appropriate for most organizations for the next five
years, possibly as much as ten. But what will be needed as we
get ready to enter the next century? Our society and economy
(both national and global) are going through a major transformation, and we are just starting to feel the initial effects.
Ferguson (1981) defines the transformation as a shift from an
economic-based paradigm to a value-based paradigm. She
describes such changes as moving from a people-to-fit-jobs,
rigid, and conforming society to a jobs-to-fit-people, flexible,
and creative environment; from aggression and competition to
cooperation and a belief that human values transcend winning;
from a time of identification with a job, organization, or pro-

126

fession to a time when identity transcends job descriptions; from an emphasis on short-term solutions to a recognition that long-range solutions must take into account harmonious work environment, employee health, and customer relations; from runaway, unbridled technology to technology used appropriately as a tool, not a tyrant; from a time of strictly economic motives and material values when progress is judged by product to a time when spiritual values will transcend material gain, when process is as important as product, and the context of work is as important as the content.

We cannot know what the actual impact of these changes will be. We believe that one reaction is already visible: the growing awareness that HRD is critical to organizational survival and productivity. We believe that HRD will continue to be increasingly more important in the future. In this chapter, we will take a final look at the HRD Effectiveness Model and present some ideas and directions that we believe HRD functions must consider to place their organizations in a positive position as we move through the predicted paradigm shifts.

The Future

What will it mean to be a responsive resource in the year 2000? It will no longer be enough for HRD functions to diagnose problems based on what is *known* in the organization or what has gone before. We must realize that we *do not know where a diagnosis may lead us.* If we solve one problem, that solution may open doors to many more. We must be open to visioning, to meditation, to many processes that today are not acceptable to HRD practice in a majority of our organizations as we seek answers to people and organizational problems. We must harness and use both hard and soft technology to solve problems as we build artificial intelligence–based expert systems to sift through the factual data, make intuitive leaps, and provide us with data bases that we can manipulate in new and different ways. Above all else, we must model openness and seeking, and acceptance of many processes known today but done in very different ways in the future. We must explore every corner of our organization and learn to use more of the available resources that we have never used before. We must be willing to fail, and fail frequently, in order to learn. We must refrain from punishing failure in those about us, and we must reach out to all the creative forces available to us in our quest.

Earlier we talked about the need for a mission statement and the role of the HRD function in helping to develop or model one. We believe that in the near future, as the paradigm shifts occur and organizations find themselves floundering between conflicting sets of values, the mission statements that support HRD will provide the life raft on which many organizations will cling for survival until the crashing waves of change have brought them into safer ports. These mission statements, crafted in this, a slightly calmer time, will provide the support and direction for HRD functions in turn to support their organizations. They must be built, and the sooner the better.

If you have demonstrated a commitment to strategic planning as part of your HRD function's ongoing output, the next step will be your *leadership* of organizational change. The effective HRD function today must be prepared for the time when it helps the organization define the parameters of change within its own context, and interprets for the organization the potential impacts of change: on people, their lives, hopes, and dreams. Today's effective HRD function is positioning itself to be technically competent in a high-tech world, to be visionary, to help workers be more autonomous and management more democratic. You must be able to lead the changes needed in your specific organization because you are competent to do so, not be dragged into the future unprepared for whatever might come.

To prepare for the future and as yet unknown roles and responsibilities means starting now to identify where you and your function will be in ten or even twenty years. It means dreaming of tasks and responsibilities and processes that cannot possibly exist today. It means thinking "outside the box"—*way outside!*

It means thinking about the things you may be doing in terms of real flexibility. It means thinking about how the things you and your staff may be doing in the workplace can be managed to fit your individual needs, whatever they may be. For the next few years you may not be able to do much more than "outside the box" thinking about what will be going on in an enriched, self-actualized work environment, but this is a critical first step in the ultimate definition of the future effective HRD function.

We believe that it will become increasingly necessary to conduct sophisticated and automated "people-free" front-end analyses—to look at the processes, tasks, jobs, work areas, and also the knowledge base that underlies them before we put people into the task or job situation. We may be approaching breakthroughs in human learning that will enable us to make enormous leaps in knowledge acquisition, and we can no longer afford to think about the delivery of job-related information in the casual and frequently shotgun way we have used so far. We must be precise in the delivery of job-related information, and we must find ways to allow people in job settings to move from the knowledge requirements of the job to truly creative developmental experiences that contribute to their own personal growth. Jobs in the future will rely more and more on judgment than on procedures. The HRD function must be more precise in the technical application of front-end analysis and evaluation, and at the same time more creative and flexible in supporting personal development. This requires a delicate balance, one that is going to be difficult to achieve.

How well future HRD functions commit to staff development will not only determine their own effectiveness, but will also affect the success of their organizations. The human resource development profession is growing and learning unevenly, in bits and starts and leaps, toward breakthroughs in human learning and understanding. Most of us barely keep up today with the bombardment of new knowledge opportunities and experiences that come our way. Without the planned and purposeful investment of staff time and organizational dollars into systematic HRD staff development activities, the HRD function of the 1990s will cease to exist, because there will be no reason for its existence. It will no longer be of use to its organization. We must plan for development, and we must locate and hire professional HRD personnel who can then be trained in the business of our business.

It may well be that the HRD function of the future will be purely "entrepreneurial," residing within an organization as the primary source of HRD expertise, but also operating as a cost center as functions do today, working for other organizations when appropriate. It may be that several of these types of HRD functions will join together in a new kind of professional HRD organization within an industry; or it may be that one HRD function will serve several related industries with a specific competency and be funded jointly by all the industries it supports. HRD functions today need to be looking at different options for supporting their organization or industry; we cannot afford to feel threatened if our organization needs for us to become a profit center, for instance. We must take the initiative to prepare ourselves, the HRD staff, and our organizations to begin to think about the optional reporting and financial relationships that will continue to place us in the asset and not the liability column.

There will always be the need for HRD functional communication to and involvement of the larger organization in training and development actions. As our organizations change and become more decentralized, flexible, and entrepreneurial, the communications effort may well become easier—but the need will remain. And it may get harder before it gets easier. In the near future, as we proceed through major changes in values as well as organizational structure, HRD functions will be hard pressed to do an effective marketing and public relations job. Organizations are going to want fixes—*now*. HRD functions may find that swamp draining is really difficult for a while, as they attempt to market to the alligators.

In a time when bottom lines seem to loom out of proportion, when we are told to cut our staff head count and produce more effective products, it is going to be crucial for HRD personnel to maintain the professionalism that will continue to mark them as experts. It has been our observation that some people achieve the "expert" reference more from their verbal skills or the competence of their staffs than their own abilities. We believe that within the next few years, the "articulate incompetent" will have been moved up and mostly out, and the effective HRD functions that survive to the year 2000 will be a collection of truly competent and creative lifetime learners. These will be people whose searching minds plan and systematically go about the process of continually developing and refining their expertise.

We have not spent as much time in this book talking about creativity and flexibility as we would have liked to; the fact is, we were disappointed that it was not as high a priority in our research data as we had hoped. It did surface, however. We believe that creativity and flexibility will become increasingly recognized as absolutely essential to an effective HRD function, not to mention essential to a successful organization. The HRD function of the future will use all sorts of flexible work schedules and environments to support staff creativity; people will be paid incentives on the basis of team productivity as well as individual expertise; teams will be drawn from HRD functions across organizations and will be linked electronically, and significant amounts of time in effective HRD functions will be spent in communication and trust-building activities, and in meaningful play: Outward Bound and "ropes" courses; electronic roundtable discussions, bulletin boards, and networks; accelerated learning experiences; games and shared simulations. We will plan for play and creativity time just as we plan for staff meetings today. We believe that the most successful HRD functions in the future will be those that play well together.

We believe that two things will happen in the next ten years: many HRD activities of the 1980s will become more and more integrated into the everyday business of successful organizations, and at the same time, successful HRD functions, while perceived as an integral "part of the business," will become more specialized in highly professional areas. For instance, line managers will assume many responsibilities now assigned to HRD personnel: coaching and counseling, and a significant amount of training in job and task-related areas. Yet computer-assisted program design is becoming more sophisticated and specialized.

To prepare for the change, HRD functions must recognize and support the migration of all the activities possible into field organizations, and at the same time must be sensitive to those highly professional areas such as needs analysis, curriculum design, and computer-based training that can best be done in a centralized professional organization. It will continue to be a matter of facilitating the hands-off style while strengthening professional expertise in specific areas for the foreseeable future.

It will continue to be necessary for HRD functions to understand, clarify, and support organizational goals and objectives. We are certain that many organizational goals and objectives will change as we move into the twenty-first century—and the HRD function may help facilitate this change.

We can only wonder if the need for the function to be perceived as conducting reality-based programs will continue to be as much of a requirement in the year 2000 as it is today for HRD effectiveness. We will no doubt be dealing with different realities at that time. The critical point is the necessity for an HRD function to meet customer needs, whether we refer to the needs of one or more larger organizations. Whatever the reality is for the organization, the HRD function should be meeting the contextual needs. Although needs will change, we do not believe this will.

Conceivably, networking with all levels of management will become easier as our organizations become more decentralized and entrepreneurial. It will also become easier as people in future organizations are encouraged to move across jobs, developing expertise in multiple disciplines. The HRD function wishing to position itself for the future will develop support processes to enable such job change and personal development.

Key Ideas for the Year 2000

Finally, we want to share with you some of our thoughts about the role that the HRD function will play in relation to two key concepts in the whole transformation drama. These concepts are change (individual and organization) and adult learning.

Change. We know today that certain changes will take place. We know that technology is becoming more sophisticated. We can predict with a high degree of certainty that organizational structures will continue to change (for instance, we know there will be fewer levels of management and more distributed and matrix-type management structures). We can even see the manager role beginning to shift from a director of people and work to a collaborator and mentor.

We have already witnessed how management in some of the new high-technology companies is considered to be another category of employees with certain special skills and responsibilities rather than employees with more responsibilities and thus more status than other employees. In these companies there are no executive parking spaces, dining halls, or restrooms. Managers and technical specialists are part of a team, with managers being responsible for coordination of the work and development of the team members.

Cooperation and teamwork are becoming more the norm than the exception. Managers will need skills in group facilitation, coaching, and counseling, as we noted earlier. If managers are to have primary responsibility for individual and group development, let us take a hard look at where that leaves HRD.

The HRD function will still need to develop managers by providing them with these new skills. More important, as the transformation intensifies, the HRD function will need to anticipate changes, to build visions. The HRD function will shift from being a *change agent* to a *change manager*. ASTD's Model of Excellence Study (1983) cites "futuring skills" as one of the critical competencies needed by training and development practitioners. Just as medical science diagnoses and treats hypertension in forty-year-olds in order to prevent heart attacks when they are sixty years old, so HRD will become increasingly responsible for diagnosing and treating *potential* problem areas before they turn into crises. The HRD function will link OD approaches to career development programs, to provide a holistic strategy of individual and organizational change. The HRD function will manage organization transformation efforts to assist the organization in dealing with change as the norm. Finally, the function will provide the counseling and expertise to help employees become self-directed learners so that they can learn to cope and live in new environments.

Adult Learning. As we move deeper into this transformation, it becomes obvious that learning will continue to be one of the most needed skills for all of us. This means all sorts of things in this changing world: computer proficiency, information management, resource identification and management, and every aspect of personal growth. Professionals with learning skills and adequate technology support will be able to keep up with changes on their own or with minimal support from HRD, but there will always be a need for face-to-face interactions to support learning and growth. HRD professionals will facilitate this personal/professional networking by playing the role of networking specialists (Stacy, Lawrence, and Hutchinson, 1983).

We have touched on the fact that people will be changing jobs and careers and moving in and out of shifting work/family/leisure patterns more and more frequently. The HRD function will provide the organizational anchor that employees will be able to turn to for support. We are not advocating that HRD professionals become therapeutic counselors (although some HRD functions do house employee assistance programs). Rather, they can provide the first line of support to link employees with more in-depth assistance. What we are advocating is the need for HRD functions to provide services to both the organization and the individual, and to have the expertise to orchestrate a blending and weaving of the priorities of each into one unified vision.

There is no doubt that we can become the future vision builders and facilitators, the transformation guides, the learning experts of the organization of tomorrow. One thing will remain the same—in order to be effective in whatever role we play, we must continue to be a responsive resource.

Learning in the Workplace of Tomorrow

Every aspect of the HRD function has the potential to become more complex in the future. We have more questions at this point than we have answers and facts. We have presented some data and some beliefs that we have derived from these data and from our experience. We would like to close this book with some of the unanswered questions, the issues, if you will, that still concern us. We hope you will join us in thinking about the implications of these issues over the next ten to twenty years.

- If more employees start working at home, what will be the impact on identifying training needs? On scheduling and delivering development activities?
- How will artificial intelligence research contribute to adult learning? (Xerox has just established an Institute for Research and Learning to study this specific question.)
- How will the next several rounds of technological advances (holographic projection, pocket TVs and telephones, libraries on line to mainframe computers, voice-activated computers) affect instruction?
- What will be the effect of robotics on the HRD field?
- How will the next evolutionary step toward a more spiritually oriented "peak performer" affect training and development?
- What will happen if we find a method of implanting learning directly into the brain?

These and other questions may seem to be just a speculative exercise, but they are the future, and we plan to be a part of it—an effective part.

> Between midnight and dawn, when sleep will not come and all the old wounds begin to ache, I often have a nightmare vision of a future world in which there are billions of people, all numbered and registered with not a gleam of genius anywhere, not an original mind, a rich personality, on the whole packaged globe. The twin ideals of our time, organization and quantity, will have won forever [J. B. Priestley, *Thoughts in the Wilderness*, 1958].

We believe that human resource development professionals have a critical responsibility to build the most effective and responsive functions possible, to ensure that such a vision can never become reality. We believe we *can* and must envision and help to create the future that will position healthy organizations for the twenty-first century.

> Enough if something from our hands have power
> To live, and act, and serve the future hour
> [William Wordsworth, "The River Duddon, Sonnet: Afterthought," 1820].

References

Alden, J. (ed.). *Critical Research Issues Facing HRD.* Alexandria, Va.: American Society for Training and Development, 1982.

American Society for Training and Development. *Serving the New Corporation.* Alexandria, Va.: American Society for Training and Development, 1986.

Bell, C. "The High Performance Trainer." *Training and Development Journal,* 1983, *37* (6), 42–45.

Bell, C. "Building a Reputation for Training Effectiveness." *Training and Development Journal,* 1984, *38* (5), 50–54.

Bové, R. "Should HRD Directors Have a Training Background?" *Training and Development Journal,* 1985, *39* (11), 28–29.

Bové, R. "What Steps Can HRD Practitioners Take to Develop Themselves Professionally?" *Training and Development Journal,* 1986, *40* (12), 22–23.

Brinkerhoff, R. "Expanding Needs Analysis." *Training and Development Journal,* 1986, *40* (2), 64–65.

Bullock, D. H. *Training Consultant's Memo,* 1981, *1* (5), 2.

Business Failure Record, 1982–1983. New York: Dun & Bradstreet, 1983.

Desatnick, R. "What Makes the Human Resource Function Successful." *Training and Development Journal,* 1984, *38* (2), 41–46.

Enright, J. "The Philosopher CEO: Plato Up-to-Date." Presentation to the American Society for Training and Development national conference, St. Louis, Mo., 1986.

Ferguson, M. *The Aquarian Conspiracy: Personal and Social Transformation in the 80's.* Los Angeles: J. P. Tarcher, 1981.

Galagan, P. "The Change Masters: Interview with Rosabeth Moss Kanter." *Training and Development Journal*, 1984, *38* (4), 39–43.

Hutcheson, P., and Stump, R. "Mining the Future." *Training and Development Journal*, 1984, *38* (11), 66–72.

Kanter, R. M. *The Change Masters*. New York: Simon & Schuster, 1983.

Kuhn, T. S. *The Structure of Scientific Revolutions*. Chicago: University of Chicago Press, 1962.

Kurlander, G. "Training Can Play Key Role in Major Organization Change." *Training Directors' Forum Newsletter*, 1986, *2* (1), 3–4.

Lee, C. "Congoleum Corporation: Training for Productivity." *Training Management*, 1983, *20* (8), 49–52.

Lee, C. "Dean Witter Reynolds: A Time for Training." *Training Magazine*, 1984a, *21* (9), 71–75.

Lee, C. "Training of the Hewlett-Packard Team." *Training Management*, 1984b, *21* (3), 24–31.

Lee, C. "Training at Loew's Corporation: If It's Not Broken. . . ." *Training Magazine*, 1985, *22* (4), 43–46.

Lippitt, G. "Criteria for Evaluating Human Resource Development." *Training and Development Journal*, 1976, *30* (10), 3–10.

Lusterman, S. *Trends in Corporate Education and Training*. New York: The Conference Board, 1985.

Miller, D. W., and Barnett, S. T. (eds.). *The How-To Handbook on: Doing Research in Human Resource Development*. Alexandria, Va.: American Society for Training and Development, 1986.

Moon, L. "Twelve Tips for Solidifying Training's Corporate Role." *Training Directors' Forum Newsletter*, 1986, *1* (3), 3.

Nadler, L. *Developing Human Resources*. San Diego, Calif.: Gulf Publishing, 1979.

"Profile: Charles Fields." *Training Directors' Forum Newsletter*, 1986, *2* (2), 6.

"Profile: Ed Robbins." *Training Directors' Forum Newsletter*, 1986, *2* (1), 6.

"Profile: Russell Young." *Training Directors' Forum Newsletter*, 1986, *2* (6), 6.

Provus, M. *Discrepancy Evaluation for Educational Improvement and Assessment.* Berkeley, Calif.: McCutchen Publishing, 1971.

Rossman, M. H., and Carey, D. M. "Adult Education and the Delphi Technique: An Explanation and Application." *Journal of Continuing Education and Training,* 1973, *2* (3), 247-252.

Rothwell, W. J. "How to Conduct a Real Performance Audit." *Training,* 1984, *21* (6), 45-49.

Rothwell, W. J. "The Case for External Peer Review." *Training and Development Journal,* 1985, *38* (6), 78.

Shoemaker, H. A. "Evaluating a Training Staff: A Case History." *Improving Human Performance Quarterly,* 1976, *5* (3-4), 183-202.

Stacy, K., Lawrence, L., and Hutchinson, F. "High-Tech/High Touch: The Future Role of HRD in the World of Work." *Training and Development Journal,* 1983, *37* (6), 132-136.

Steele, S. M. *Contemporary Approaches to Program Evaluation and Their Implications for Evaluating Programs for Disadvantaged Adults.* Syracuse, N.Y.: ERIC Clearinghouse on Adult Education, Syracuse University, 1973.

Tersine, R. J., and Riggs, W. E. "The Delphi Technique: A Long-Range Planning Tool." *Business Horizons,* 1976, *19* (2), 51-56.

Tracey, W. R. *Managing Training and Development Systems.* New York: AMACOM, 1974.

Zenger, J. H., and Blitzer, R. J. "How Training Managers Become Corporate Heroes/Heroines." *Training Magazine,* 1981, *18* (11), 22-23.

Index

Index